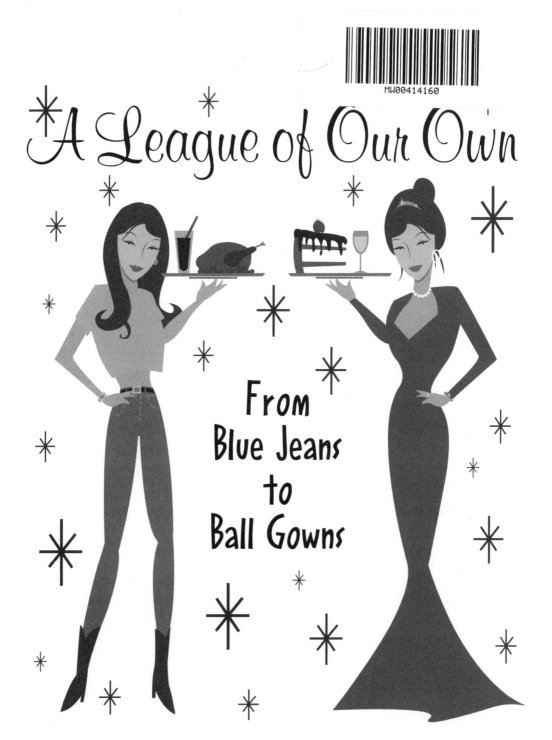

A League of Our Own

From Blue Jeans to Ball Gowns

All-Occasion Recipes from the Rockwall Women's League

A League of Our Own

From Blue Jeans to Ball Gowns
All-Occasion Recipes from the Rockwall Women's League

Published by Rockwall Women's League
Copyright © 2006 by
Rockwall Women's League
P.O. Box 383
Rockwall, Texas 75087

Graphics designed by Qball Design.

ISBN 0-9766317-0-9

Edited and Manufactured by

CommunityClassics™

An imprint of

FRP™

P.O. Box 305142
Nashville, Tennessee 37230
(800) 358-0560

Manufactured in China
4,000 copies

Proceeds from the sale of this cookbook will be returned to the community through projects and organizations supported by the Rockwall Women's League.

A League of Our Own

Whenever two or more women gather together, something is always "cooking!" It may be volunteering on a service project, sharing a new recipe at the monthly meeting, or hosting guests at the annual charity ball. Whether in blue jeans or ball gowns, or something in between, the ladies of the Rockwall Women's League serve their community.

Recipes in this collection reflect the diverse personalities and lifestyles of our membership. This all-occasion book was assembled with quick and easy family favorites along with more challenging current culinary trends to appeal to the novice cook as well as to the gourmet chef. By exploring this tempting assortment of recipes, you will certainly enhance your own creative menus.

We are happy to present our second Rockwall Women's League cookbook and anticipate future years of fine cuisine, lifelong friendships, and service to the Rockwall area.

This cookbook is dedicated to women of integrity everywhere who serve their communities.

Mission Statement
Rockwall Women's League

The commitment of the Rockwall Women's League is to unite and promote the Rockwall area through service to the community and through the initiation and support of civic, educational, and social events.

History

In early 1973, Rockwall, Texas, was at the beginning of a change. A twenty-two mile drive east of downtown Dallas placed you by the newly formed Lake Ray Hubbard. People were discovering the charm of a lakeside community with a hometown atmosphere for raising a family. Rockwall Women's League was chartered with fifty members in November 1973 to unite and serve the growing community. The club's membership now stands at eighty active members, seventy-six associate members, and six founding members with honorary status.

The annual charity ball with its different theme each year is the club's primary means of raising funds for service projects. This black-tie gala, generously supported by the individuals and businesses of Rockwall, enables the league to provide substantial scholarships to graduating seniors and to donate money to many service-oriented organizations in the community.

A general business meeting, followed by a program, is held the second Friday of each month from September through May. Prospective members and their guests are welcome. For more information, please write to:

Rockwall Women's League
P.O. Box 383
Rockwall, Texas 75087
www.rockwallwomensleague.org

"We make a living by what we do, but we make a life by what we give."

— Winston Churchill

Table of Contents

Appetizers & Aperitifs

Breakfast, Brunch & Breads

Sumptuous Soups & Salads

Elegant Entrées

Vegetables & Sides

166

Decadent Desserts

188

"Small cheer and great welcome makes
a merry feast."

—William Shakespeare

Appetizers & Aperitifs

Party Salsa

1 (15-ounce) can black beans
1 (15-ounce) can black-eyed peas
1 (15-ounce) can Shoe Peg corn
2 (14^1/$_2$-ounce) cans diced tomatoes
1 bunch green onions, chopped
1 green bell pepper, chopped
^{1}/$_2$ cup chopped cilantro
1 (8-ounce) bottle Zesty Italian salad dressing

Pour the black beans, black-eyed peas, corn and tomatoes into a colander. Rinse and drain well. Remove to a large bowl. Add the green onions, bell pepper, cilantro and salad dressing and toss to mix. Cover and marinate in the refrigerator for at least 8 hours. Drain off excess liquid and serve with tortilla chips. **Makes 8 cups.**

Black Bean Salsa with Citrus Dressing

2 (15-ounce) cans black beans, rinsed and drained
1 (6-ounce) can mandarin oranges, drained
^{1}/$_2$ small purple onion, chopped
1 large green bell pepper, chopped
1 (15-ounce) can whole kernel corn, drained
1 tablespoon chopped pickled jalapeño chile
^{1}/$_4$ cup vegetable oil
^{1}/$_4$ cup red wine vinegar
^{1}/$_3$ to ^{1}/$_2$ cup orange juice
^{1}/$_4$ teaspoon salt

Combine the black beans, oranges, onion, bell pepper, corn and jalapeño in a large bowl. Whisk the oil, vinegar, orange juice and salt in a small bowl. Drizzle over the black bean mixture and toss to coat. **Makes 8 cups.**

"To-Die-For" Dip

16 ounces cream cheese, softened

1 cup sour cream

1 (1-ounce) package ranch salad dressing mix

1 (7-ounce) can Mexicorn

1 (2^1/$_4$-ounce) can chopped or sliced black olives in jalapeño juice

^{1}/$_2$ green bell pepper, chopped

Combine the cream cheese, sour cream, salad dressing mix, corn, olives with juice and bell pepper in a bowl. Stir to mix well. Serve with your favorite crackers or chips. **Makes 4 cups.**

Fabulously Easy Corn and Jalapeño Dip

8 ounces cream cheese

^{1}/$_2$ cup (1 stick) margarine

1 (15^1/$_4$-ounce) can whole kernel corn, drained

4 to 5 pickled jalapeño chiles, finely chopped

Combine the cream cheese, margarine, corn and jalapeños in a microwave-safe bowl. Microwave until the cream cheese and margarine melt, stirring occasionally. Serve with corn chips. **Makes 2 cups.**

Jammin' Dip

1 cup toasted chopped pecans

1/4 cup mayonnaise

1 cup shredded Cheddar cheese

1/2 cup chopped green onions

Hot pepper jelly or chipotle sauce

Combine the pecans, mayonnaise, cheese and green onions in a bowl. Stir to mix well. Cover and chill overnight. Shape into a log and place on a serving plate. Cover with the hot pepper jelly and serve with crackers. **Serves 8 to 10.**

Chutney Cheese Dip

8 ounces cream cheese, softened

2 tablespoons sour cream

2 teaspoons curry powder

1/2 cup chopped green onions

1/2 cup raisins

1/2 cup coarsely chopped dry-roasted peanuts

1 cup chutney

Combine the cream cheese, sour cream, curry powder, green onions, raisins, peanuts and chutney in a bowl. Stir to mix well. Cover and chill overnight. Serve with crackers. **Makes 3 cups.**

Spicy Hummus

6 cups garbanzo beans, rinsed and drained

1 rounded tablespoon cumin

2 tablespoons honey

$^1/_2$ cup lemon juice

$^1/_2$ cup tahini

1 cup olive oil

$^1/_3$ cup fresh cilantro, chopped

2 (or more) chipotle chiles in sauce

Salt and pepper to taste

Purée the garbanzo beans in a food processor fitted with a steel blade. Add the cumin, honey, lemon juice, tahini, olive oil, cilantro and chiles with sauce. Season with salt and pepper. Process until well mixed. Remove to a bowl. Cover and chill overnight. Serve with crackers or toasted pita wedges. **Makes 6 cups.**

Yankee Beef Dip

8 ounces cream cheese, softened

2 cups sour cream

1 (2¼-ounce) jar sliced dried beef, finely chopped

½ yellow onion, finely chopped

½ green bell pepper, finely chopped

1 (4-ounce) package slivered almonds

Mix the cream cheese and sour cream in a bowl. Add the dried beef, onion and bell pepper. Stir to mix well. Spoon into a baking dish. Bake at 350 degrees for 20 minutes. Sprinkle with the almonds and serve warm with crackers. **Serves 12.**

Chicken Enchilada Dip

¼ cup (½ stick) butter

¾ cup chopped onion

2 (12½-ounce) cans chicken

1 (7-ounce) can diced green chiles

2 (10¾-ounce) cans condensed cream of chicken soup

2 cups crushed tortilla chips

1 cup shredded Cheddar cheese

Garlic powder to taste

1 cup shredded Cheddar cheese

Melt the butter in a skillet. Add the onion and sauté until tender. Remove to a large bowl. Add the chicken, green chiles, soup, tortilla chips and 1 cup cheese. Season with garlic powder. Stir to mix well. Spoon into a 9×13-inch baking dish. Top with 1 cup cheese. Bake at 350 degrees for 30 minutes. Serve with tortilla chips. **Serves 18.**

Hot Crab Dip

8 ounces cream cheese, softened
1 (6-ounce) can crab meat, drained
1 heaping tablespoon mayonnaise or salad dressing
2 green onions, chopped
1 tablespoon horseradish
Dash of Tabasco sauce
Dash of salt
Dash of pepper

Combine the cream cheese, crab meat, mayonnaise, green onions, horseradish, Tabasco sauce, salt and pepper in a bowl. Stir to mix well. Spoon into a baking dish. Bake at 400 degrees for 15 minutes. Serve hot with crackers. **Makes about 2 cups.**

Salmon Mousse

8 ounces cream cheese, softened
1 tablespoon horseradish
1 tablespoon lemon juice
1 tablespoon finely chopped onion
1 tablespoon liquid smoke
1/4 teaspoon salt
1 (16-ounce) can high-quality red salmon, drained and flaked
Capers, rinsed and drained

Combine the cream cheese, horseradish, lemon juice, onion, liquid smoke and salt in a food processor. Process until well mixed and creamy. Remove to a bowl. Stir in the salmon and capers. Cover and chill for 12 hours. Garnish with fresh parsley and serve with assorted crackers. **Serves 12.**

Basil Parmesan Spread

8 ounces cream cheese, softened
4 ounces fresh goat cheese
1 (10-ounce) jar basil pesto
3 ounces fresh Parmesan cheese, grated

$1/4$ cup finely chopped walnuts
1 (8-ounce) jar sun-dried tomatoes,
  drained and chopped

Mix the cream cheese and goat cheese in a bowl until smooth. Spread $1/3$ of the cream cheese mixture in the bottom of a small bowl lined with plastic wrap. Spread with $1/2$ of the pesto. Sprinkle with $1/2$ of the Parmesan cheese and $1/2$ of the walnuts. Top with $1/2$ of the tomatoes. Repeat the layers with $1/3$ of the cream cheese mixture and the remaining pesto, Parmesan cheese, walnuts and tomatoes. Spread with the remaining $1/3$ of the cream cheese mixture. Cover with plastic wrap and chill overnight. Invert onto a serving plate and surround with crackers. Let stand at room temperature for 30 minutes before serving. **Serves 12.**

Homemade Boursin Cheese

8 ounces cream cheese, softened
$1/3$ cup sour cream
$1/4$ cup ($1/2$ stick) butter, softened
1 garlic clove, minced
1 tablespoon dried chives

1 tablespoon fresh parsley
$1/4$ teaspoon thyme
$1/4$ teaspoon dillweed
Salt and pepper to taste

Combine the cream cheese, sour cream, butter, garlic, chives, parsley, thyme and dillweed in a food processor fitted with a steel blade. Season with salt and pepper. Process until well mixed. Remove to a crock and cover. Chill until firm. Serve with crackers. **Serves 8.**

Marinated Cheese

$1/2$ cup olive oil

$1/2$ cup white wine vinegar

3 tablespoons chopped fresh parsley

3 tablespoons finely chopped green onions

1 teaspoon sugar

$3/4$ teaspoon basil

$1/2$ teaspoon salt

$1/2$ teaspoon pepper

3 garlic cloves, minced

1 (2-ounce) jar diced pimentos, drained

1 (8-ounce) package cream cheese, cut into $1/4$-inch slices

1 (8-ounce) block sharp Cheddar cheese, cut into $1/4$-inch slices

Whisk the olive oil, vinegar, parsley, green onions, sugar, basil, salt, pepper, garlic and pimentos in a bowl. Place the cream cheese slices on the Cheddar cheese slices. Arrange on a large serving platter, alternating the cream cheese and Cheddar cheese side up. Pour the marinade over the cheese. Cover and chill for at least 8 hours. **Serves 12.**

Teacher's Favorite "Apple" Cheese Ball

8 ounces sharp white Cheddar cheese, shredded

8 ounces regular cream cheese or reduced-fat cream cheese, softened

4 (or more) garlic cloves, chopped

$1/8$ teaspoon ground red pepper

Paprika

1 cinnamon stick

1 bay leaf

Combine the Cheddar cheese, cream cheese, garlic and ground red pepper in a food processor fitted with a metal blade. Process until well mixed. Remove to a bowl and chill for 30 minutes. Shape into a ball and make an indentation on the top to resemble an apple. Chill for 30 minutes. Coat completely with paprika and place on a serving plate. Insert the cinnamon stick and bay leaf in the indentation to resemble an apple stem and leaf. Chill for at least 2 hours. Serve with water crackers or wheat crackers. **Serves 10.**

Spicy Cheese Ring

10 ounces sharp Cheddar cheese, shredded

10 ounces mild Cheddar cheese, shredded

3/4 teaspoon cayenne pepper

2 teaspoons finely chopped onion

1 cup mayonnaise

1/2 cup walnuts, chopped

Lettuce leaves

Chopped walnuts

1 jar strawberry preserves

Mix the sharp Cheddar cheese and mild Cheddar cheese in a large bowl. Add the cayenne pepper, onion and mayonnaise and stir to mix well. Sprinkle 1/2 cup walnuts in the bottom of an oiled 4-cup ring mold. Pack the cheese mixture into the mold. Cover and chill overnight. Arrange lettuce leaves on a serving plate. Unmold the cheese mixture onto the lettuce leaves. Sprinkle with additional chopped walnuts. Spoon the strawberry preserves into the center. Serve with crackers. **Serves 24.**

Jalapeño and Pimento Squares

4 cups shredded Cheddar cheese

4 eggs, beaten

3 canned jalapeño chiles, chopped

1 (2-ounce) jar diced pimentos, drained

1 teaspoon finely chopped onion

Combine the cheese, eggs, jalapeños, pimentos and onion in a bowl. Stir to mix well. Spread in a lightly greased 8×8-inch baking pan. Bake at 350 degrees for 30 to 40 minutes. Remove to a wire rack to cool. Cut into squares. **Serves 16.**

Baked Cream Cheese

1 (8-ounce) can refrigerator crescent rolls

1 (8-ounce) block cream cheese

1/2 teaspoon dillweed

1 egg yolk, beaten

Unroll the crescent dough on a lightly floured work surface. Press the seams to seal and form a 4×12-inch rectangle. Sprinkle the top of the cream cheese with 1/2 of the dillweed. Press the dillweed lightly into the cream cheese. Place, dill side down, in the center of the dough. Sprinkle with the remaining dillweed. Enclose the cream cheese in the dough and press the sides to seal. Place on a lightly greased baking sheet. Brush with the egg yolk. Bake at 350 degrees for 15 to 18 minutes. Serve with crackers. **Serves 8 to 10.**

Savory Parmesan Bites

8 ounces cream cheese, softened

1 cup grated Parmesan cheese

2 (8-ounce) cans refrigerator crescent rolls

1 cup finely chopped red bell pepper

$^1/_4$ cup chopped chives or green onions

Beat the cream cheese and Parmesan cheese in a bowl with an electric mixer at medium speed until well blended. Unroll the crescent dough on a lightly floured surface to form two 4×12-inch rectangles. Press the seams to seal. Spread $^1/_2$ of the cream cheese mixture over the surface of 1 rectangle of dough. Sprinkle with $^1/_2$ of the bell pepper and $^1/_2$ of the chives. Repeat with the remaining dough, cream cheese mixture, bell pepper and chives. Roll up the dough lengthwise. Wrap the rolls in plastic wrap and chill for 4 hours. Remove the plastic wrap and cut the rolls into $^1/_2$-inch slices. Place 1 inch apart on a nonstick baking sheet. Bake at 350 degrees for 13 to 15 minutes or until golden brown. Remove to a wire rack and let cool slightly. Serve warm. **Serves 32.**

Sausage Cups

1 pound hot bulk pork sausage

1 pound fresh mushrooms, finely chopped

4 green onions, finely chopped

8 ounces cream cheese

Salt and pepper to taste

3 (15-count) packages mini phyllo shells

Brown the sausage in a skillet, stirring until crumbly; drain. Add the mushrooms and green onions and sauté until the vegetables are tender. Add the cream cheese. Cook until the cream cheese melts, stirring often. Season with salt and pepper. Spoon into the phyllo shells and arrange on a nonstick baking sheet. Bake at 350 degrees for 10 to 15 minutes. **Serves 45.**

Note: These may be made ahead and frozen.

Sausage Grab-its

1 pound bulk pork sausage

2 (5-ounce) jars Old English cheese spread

2 tablespoons margarine

^{1}/2 teaspoon garlic powder

^{1}/2 teaspoon red pepper flakes

5 or 6 English muffins, split

Brown the sausage in a skillet, stirring until crumbly; drain. Stir in the cheese spread, margarine, garlic powder and red pepper flakes. Cook until the cheese and margarine melt, stirring often. Spoon onto the muffin halves and arrange on a baking sheet. Broil until bubbly. Cut each muffin half into quarters, if desired. **Makes 10 or 12 halves.**

Ham and Cheese Party Sandwiches

30 Hawaiian-style rolls or other 2-inch bakery-style rolls
2 pounds shaved deli ham
1 pound Monterey Jack cheese, shredded
1 cup (2 sticks) butter
2 tablespoons mustard
2 teaspoons Worcestershire sauce

Slice the rolls in half. Place the ham and cheese on the rolls to make sandwiches. Arrange the sandwiches in a 9×13-inch baking dish. Melt the butter in a saucepan. Stir in the mustard and Worcestershire sauce. Pour evenly over the sandwiches. Cover and chill overnight. Bake, covered, at 350 degrees for 20 minutes or until the cheese melts. **Serves 30.**

Side Door Quesadillas

Olive oil
8 large flour tortillas
2 cups cubed grilled chicken
1 cup chopped pecans
1 cup thinly sliced green onions
2 cups shredded sharp Cheddar cheese
1 cup cubed Gorgonzola cheese
2 ripe pears, cored and thinly sliced

Brush olive oil on 1 side of each tortilla. Lay 4 tortillas, oiled side down, on a work surface. Top each with the chicken, pecans, green onions, Cheddar cheese, Gorgonzola cheese and pears. Top each with a tortilla, oiled side up. Cook the quesadillas in a skillet over medium heat until golden brown on both sides and the cheese is slightly melted. Remove to a cutting board and cut each quesadilla into quarters. **Serves 16.**

Jalapeño Wrap-Ups

6 boneless chicken breasts, cut into 50 small strips

25 fresh jalapeño chiles, halved lengthwise and partially seeded

1 pound bacon, each slice cut into thirds

$1/2$ cup soy sauce

$1/4$ cup Worcestershire sauce

$1/4$ cup vegetable oil

Place 1 chicken strip into each jalapeño half. Wrap 1 piece of bacon around each jalapeño and secure with a wooden pick. Arrange in a shallow dish. Whisk the soy sauce, Worcestershire sauce and oil in a small bowl. Pour over the jalapeños. Cover and chill overnight. Remove the jalapeños from the marinade and grill or broil for 7 minutes per side. Wrap in foil and place in a 350-degree oven if necessary to finish cooking the chicken. Serve warm with plenty of water to drink. **Makes 50.**

Shrimp Ceviche

1 pound fresh deveined peeled shrimp

2 tablespoons Cajun seasoning

3 tablespoons butter

$^1/_2$ onion, finely chopped

$^1/_3$ cup chopped fresh cilantro

$^1/_2$ cup ketchup

2 tablespoons bottled Mexican hot sauce, such as Tamazula

2 tablespoons (about) olive oil

1 cup diced peeled cucumber

2 tablespoons vodka

$^1/_2$ teaspoon (about) salt

1 small avocado, pitted and cubed

Combine the shrimp and Cajun seasoning in a bowl. Toss to coat. Melt the butter in a skillet. Add the shrimp and sauté for 4 minutes or until the shrimp turn pink; do not overcook. Remove to a bowl and let cool. Rinse the chopped onion in cold water and drain well. Add to the shrimp. Add the cilantro, ketchup, hot sauce, olive oil, cucumber and vodka. Stir gently to mix. Stir in the salt. Taste and add more salt, if desired. Cover and chill for a few hours. Stir in the avocado. Spoon into martini glasses or small bowls. Garnish with lime slices and serve with tortilla chips. **Makes 6 cups or serves 6.**

Barbecue Shrimp Cocktail

2 cups cooked corn kernels

1 cup (1/4-inch diced) jicama

1/4 cup (1/4-inch diced) red onion

1/4 cup (1/4-inch diced) red bell pepper

2 tablespoons finely chopped fresh cilantro

2 tablespoons freshly squeezed lime juice

Salt and pepper to taste

12 deveined peeled jumbo fresh shrimp

1/4 cup olive oil

3 tablespoons barbecue spice mix or other good dry rub spice mix

1 head romaine, rinsed, dried and shredded

1/2 cup salad dressing of your choice

1/4 cup sour cream

1/2 cup fresh cilantro sprigs

Combine the corn, jicama, onion, bell pepper, 2 tablespoons chopped cilantro and lime juice in a bowl. Season with salt and pepper. Toss to mix. Cover and chill for several hours. Drizzle the shrimp with the olive oil in a bowl. Sprinkle with the spice mix and toss to coat. Cover and chill for several hours. Combine the romaine, corn mixture and salad dressing in a bowl. Toss to mix. Spoon into four 8-ounce martini glasses. Grill or sauté the shrimp until the shrimp turn pink. Place 3 cooked shrimp over the rim of each martini glass. Top each glass with 1 tablespoon sour cream and cilantro sprigs. **Serves 4.**

Shrimp Appetizers

1 (4-ounce) can deveined baby shrimp
1 (5-ounce) jar Old English cheese spread
1 tablespoon mayonnaise
$1/2$ cup (1 stick) butter, softened
$1/2$ teaspoon salt
$1/2$ teaspoon garlic powder
14 English muffins

Mix the shrimp, cheese spread, mayonnaise, butter, salt and garlic powder in a microwave-safe bowl. Microwave for 60 seconds and stir. Spread on the muffins. Freeze for 15 minutes. Cut each muffin into quarters and arrange on a nonstick baking sheet. Bake at 400 degrees for 15 minutes. **Makes 56.**

Whitford Inn Soused Shrimp

3 pounds store-cooked shrimp

$^1/_2$ bag shrimp/crab boil

2 cups thinly sliced onions

7 bay leaves

$1^1/_4$ cups vegetable oil

$^3/_4$ cup white vinegar

$1^1/_2$ teaspoons salt

$2^1/_2$ teaspoons celery seeds

$2^1/_2$ tablespoons capers

Dash of Tabasco sauce

1 (16-ounce) can button mushrooms, drained

1 (14-ounce) can artichoke hearts, drained

1 lemon, thinly sliced

Add the shrimp and shrimp boil to a large saucepan of boiling water. Cook for 1 minute and plunge into ice water for 3 minutes. Remove to a colander to drain. Stir the onions, bay leaves, oil, vinegar, salt, celery seeds, capers, Tabasco sauce, mushrooms, artichokes and lemon slices in a large bowl. Add the shrimp and stir to coat. Cover and chill for 24 hours. Remove the bay leaves. Serve in Bibb lettuce cups or with wooden picks. **Serves 30.**

Lime-Mint Tea

  4 cups water

  6 tea bags

  2 cups loosely packed fresh mint leaves, chopped

  $4^1/_2$ cups water

  $1^1/_2$ cups sugar

  $1^1/_4$ cups lemon juice

  $^1/_3$ cup fresh lime juice

Bring 4 cups water to a boil in a saucepan. Pour over the tea bags in a bowl. Cover and let steep for 5 minutes. Remove and discard the tea bags. Stir in the mint and let stand for 15 minutes. Pour the tea through a wire-mesh strainer into a bowl. Discard the mint. Bring $4^1/_2$ cups water and the sugar to a boil in a large saucepan, stirring occasionally. Remove from the heat and let cool. Stir in the tea, lemon juice and lime juice. Chill until cold. Serve over ice. **Serves 10.**

Lemon Almond Iced Tea

  2 cups water

  3 tablespoons lemon-flavored instant tea mix

  2 cups cold water

  1 (12-ounce) can frozen lemonade concentrate, thawed

  1 tablespoon vanilla extract

  1 tablespoon almond extract

  2 quarts cold water

Bring 2 cups water and the tea mix to a boil in a large saucepan. Remove from the heat and let stand for 5 minutes. Stir in 2 cups cold water, the lemonade concentrate, vanilla and almond extract. Stir in 2 quarts cold water when ready to serve and pour over ice. **Serves 12.**

Citrus Punch for 75

Ginger ale
Red food color
6 (46-ounce) cans pineapple juice
13$\frac{1}{2}$ quarts cold water
6 (12-ounce) cans frozen orange juice concentrate
6 (12-ounce) cans frozen lemonade concentrate
1$\frac{1}{2}$ teaspoons almond extract

Mix ginger ale with a few drops of food color in a bowl. Pour into a ring mold. Freeze until firm. Pour the pineapple juice into a large punch bowl. Add the water, orange juice concentrate, lemonade concentrate and almond extract. Stir until the fruit concentrates melt. Unmold the frozen ginger ale and float in the punch bowl. **Serves 75.**

Hot Cranberry Punch

2 cups cranberry juice cocktail
2$\frac{1}{2}$ cups pineapple juice
$\frac{1}{2}$ cup water
2 teaspoons whole allspice
2 teaspoons whole cloves
2 cinnamon sticks
$\frac{1}{3}$ cup packed brown sugar

Pour the cranberry juice cocktail, pineapple juice and water into the base of a coffee percolator. Place the allspice, cloves and cinnamon sticks in the clean basket and set in the percolator. Percolate until hot. Discard the spices. Add the brown sugar to the hot juice and stir until dissolved. Serve hot. **Serves 10 to 12.**

Champagne Party Punch

1 (750-milliliter) bottle Champagne
1 (750-milliliter) bottle sauterne
1 quart sparkling water
1/2 cup bourbon
Frozen ice ring

Combine the Champagne, sauterne, sparkling water and bourbon in a large punch bowl. Stir gently to mix. Float the ice ring in the punch. **Serves 20.**

Eggnog Punch

2 quarts purchased eggnog
1/4 cup packed brown sugar
2 tablespoons instant coffee granules
1/3 teaspoon cinnamon
1 cup brandy
1/3 cup coffee liqueur
1 cup heavy whipping cream
3 tablespoons confectioners' sugar
1 teaspoon vanilla extract
Cinnamon

Beat the eggnog, brown sugar, coffee granules and 1/3 teaspoon cinnamon in a bowl with an electric mixer at low speed until the coffee granules dissolve. Stir in the brandy and liqueur. Chill for 2 hours. Pour into a punch bowl. Beat the cream, confectioners' sugar and vanilla in a bowl until soft peaks form. Dollop the whipped cream on top of the punch and sprinkle with cinnamon. **Serves 10 to 12.**

Brandy Slush

7 cups water

1¹/₂ cups sugar

2 cups water

4 family-size tea bags

1 (12-ounce) can frozen orange juice concentrate, thawed

1 (12-ounce) can frozen lemonade concentrate, thawed

2¹/₂ cups peach or apricot brandy

Lemon-lime soda

Combine 7 cups water and the sugar in a saucepan. Bring to a boil and boil for 10 minutes. Remove from the heat and let cool. Bring 2 cups water to a boil in a small saucepan. Remove from the heat and add the tea bags. Cover and let cool. Remove and discard the tea bags. Combine the tea and sugar water in a sealable freezer-proof container. Stir in the orange juice concentrate and lemonade concentrate. Add the peach brandy and stir to mix well. Seal the container and freeze for 2 to 3 days, stirring daily. Spoon 2 parts slush into a glass and top with 1 part lemon-lime soda. **Makes 1 gallon.**

Note: Decaffeinated tea and/or diet soda can be used in this recipe.

Bloody Bull

2 (10^1/$_2$-ounce) cans double-strength beef stock

2 (11^1/$_2$-ounce) cans Snap•E•Tom or spicy tomato juice cocktail

2^1/$_2$ cups plus 2 tablespoons vodka

^{3}/$_4$ cup lemon juice or lime juice

2 teaspoons dried minced onion

2 teaspoons seasoned salt

1 teaspoon dillweed

1 teaspoon pepper

1 teaspoon Tabasco sauce

1 teaspoon Worcestershire sauce

Mix the beef stock, tomato juice cocktail, vodka, lemon juice, dried onion, seasoned salt, dillweed, pepper, Tabasco sauce and Worcestershire sauce in a large glass pitcher. Cover and chill for at least 7 hours. Stir and serve over ice. **Serves 18.**

Infamous Margaritas

1 (6-ounce) can frozen limeade concentrate
$2/3$ cup tequila
$1/3$ cup Triple Sec
$1/3$ cup Key lime juice

Combine the limeade concentrate, tequila, Triple Sec and lime juice in a blender. Add ice to the top of the container. Process until smooth. **Serves 6.**

Mama's Velvet Hammer

Vanilla ice cream
$1/2$ cup crème de cacao
$1/2$ cup coffee liqueur

Fill a blender with vanilla ice cream. Add the crème de cacao and coffee liqueur. Process until smooth. Serve in decorative glasses. **Serves 4.**

"This recipe is certainly silly. It says to separate two eggs, but it doesn't say how far apart to put them."

—Gracie Allen

Breakfast, Brunch & Breads

Sausage Pecan Morning Casserole

1 (16-ounce) loaf raisin bread, cubed

8 ounces bulk pork sausage, cooked and drained

6 eggs

$1^1/2$ cups milk

$1^1/2$ cups half-and-half

1 teaspoon vanilla extract

$^1/4$ teaspoon nutmeg

$^1/4$ teaspoon cinnamon

1 cup packed brown sugar

1 cup coarsely chopped pecans

$^1/2$ cup (1 stick) butter or margarine, softened

2 tablespoons maple syrup

Mix the bread and cooked sausage in a 9×13-inch baking dish coated with nonstick cooking spray. Beat the eggs, milk, half-and-half, vanilla, nutmeg and cinnamon in a bowl. Pour over the sausage mixture. Cover and chill for 8 hours or overnight. Combine the brown sugar, pecans, butter and maple syrup in a bowl. Mix until crumbly. Spoon evenly over the sausage mixture. Bake, uncovered, at 350 degrees for 35 to 40 minutes or until a knife inserted in the center comes out clean. **Serves 8 to 10.**

Sausage Crescents

1 pound seasoned bulk pork sausage

8 ounces cream cheese, softened

2 (8-ounce) cans refrigerator crescent rolls

1 egg white, lightly beaten

Poppy seeds

Brown the sausage in a skillet, stirring until crumbly; drain. Add the cream cheese and remove from the heat. Stir until the cream cheese melts and the mixture is creamy. Let cool completely. Separate the crescent dough into two 4×12-inch rectangles on a lightly floured work surface. Press the seams to seal. Spoon $^1/_2$ of the sausage mixture down the center of 1 rectangle of dough. Fold the dough lengthwise over the sausage mixture to seal. Place seam-side down on an ungreased baking sheet. Repeat with the remaining dough and sausage mixture. Brush the rolls with egg white and sprinkle lightly with poppy seeds. Bake at 350 degrees for 20 minutes or until golden brown. Remove to a wire rack and let cool slightly. Cut into $1^1/_2$-inch slices and serve warm. **Serves 18.**

Note: These can be made ahead and frozen. Reheat before serving.

Green Chile Egg Puff

10 eggs

$^1/_2$ cup all-purpose flour

1 teaspoon baking powder

$^3/_4$ teaspoon salt

12 ounces Monterey Jack cheese, shredded

1 (12-ounce) carton cottage cheese

2 (4-ounce) cans chopped green chiles

1 pound bulk pork sausage, cooked and drained (optional)

Beat the eggs in a large bowl until thick and pale yellow. Beat in the flour, baking powder and salt. Stir in the Monterey Jack cheese, cottage cheese, green chiles and crumbled sausage. Pour into a greased 9×13-inch baking dish. Bake at 350 degrees for 30 to 40 minutes. **Serves 10 to 12.**

Egg and Italian Sausage Casserole

1 pound bulk pork Italian sausage

$^1/_2$ cup chopped green onions

2 garlic cloves, minced

$^1/_2$ cup chopped sun-dried tomatoes

$^1/_4$ cup chopped fresh parsley

5 eggs

3 egg yolks

1 cup half-and-half

1 cup heavy cream

$^1/_2$ teaspoon salt

$^1/_2$ teaspoon pepper

2 cups shredded mozzarella cheese

Brown the sausage in a skillet, stirring until crumbly; drain. Add the green onions, garlic, tomatoes and parsley. Sauté until the tomatoes are tender. Spread in a greased 9×13-inch baking dish. Whisk the eggs, egg yolks, half-and-half, cream, salt and pepper in a bowl. Stir in $1^1/_2$ cups of the cheese. Pour over the sausage mixture. Sprinkle with the remaining $^1/_2$ cup cheese. Bake at 350 degrees for 30 to 40 minutes. **Serves 10 to 12.**

Ham and Cheese Soufflé

4 slices ham

4 slices Cheddar cheese

8 slices bread, crusts removed

3 eggs

1 1/2 cups milk

1/4 teaspoon dry mustard

1/4 teaspoon seasoned salt

1/4 cup (1/2 stick) butter, melted

1/4 cup crushed potato chips

Place 1 slice of ham and 1 slice of cheese between 2 slices of bread to make a sandwich. Repeat with the remaining ham, cheese and bread. Fit the sandwiches in a single layer in a 10×10-inch baking dish. Beat the eggs, milk, dry mustard and seasoned salt in a bowl. Pour evenly over the sandwiches. Cover and chill overnight. Drizzle with the melted butter and sprinkle with the crushed potato chips. Bake, covered, at 350 degrees for 1 hour. **Serves 4.**

Ham and Egg Casserole

8 hard-cooked eggs, finely chopped
1 1/2 cups chopped lean ham
1 tablespoon finely chopped fresh parsley
1/4 cup (1/2 stick) butter
1 cup cracker crumbs
1/4 cup (1/2 stick) butter
3 tablespoons all-purpose flour
2 cups milk
1/8 teaspoon pepper

Mix the eggs, ham and parsley in a bowl. Melt 1/4 cup butter in a skillet over medium heat. Add the cracker crumbs and sauté until the crumbs are golden brown. Remove from the heat. Remove and reserve a few tablespoons of the crumbs. Melt 1/4 cup butter in a saucepan over medium heat. Stir in the flour and cook until smooth, stirring constantly. Stir in the milk and pepper gradually. Cook until thickened, stirring constantly. Remove from the heat. Spread 1/3 of the cracker crumbs in the bottom of a buttered casserole dish. Sprinkle with 1/3 of the ham mixture. Pour 1/3 of the cream sauce evenly over the top. Repeat the layers 2 more times. Sprinkle with the reserved crumbs. Bake at 350 degrees for 25 minutes or until golden brown. Serve immediately.
Serves 6.

Bayou Bend Brunch Casserole

$1/2$ loaf French bread, torn into small pieces

3 tablespoon butter, melted

1 pound Monterey Jack cheese, shredded

$1/3$ pound Genoa salami, cut into thin strips

10 eggs

$1^{1}/2$ cups milk

$1/3$ cup white wine

3 large green onions, finely chopped

2 teaspoons Dijon mustard

$1/4$ teaspoon black pepper

$1/8$ teaspoon red pepper flakes

1 cup sour cream

$1/2$ cup grated fresh Parmesan cheese

Spread the bread in a well-greased 9×13-inch baking dish and drizzle with the melted butter. Sprinkle with the Monterey Jack cheese and salami. Beat the eggs, milk, wine, green onions, mustard, black pepper and red pepper flakes in a bowl until frothy. Pour over the bread mixture. Cover with foil and chill overnight. Let stand at room temperature for 30 minutes before baking. Bake, covered, at 325 degrees for 1 hour. Spread the sour cream over the top and sprinkle with the Parmesan cheese. Bake, uncovered, for 10 minutes longer or until light brown. **Serves 12.**

Simply Elegant Eggs

4 English muffins, split and toasted
8 (¹/4-inch-thick) slices Canadian bacon
8 poached eggs
1¹/2 cups pasteurized process cheese spread
¹/4 cup milk

Arrange the muffin halves in a 9×13-inch baking dish. Top each with a slice of bacon and a poached egg. Cover and chill. Combine the cheese spread and milk in a saucepan. Cook until hot, stirring constantly. Pour over the eggs. Bake at 350 degrees for 20 minutes. Serve garnished with parsley sprigs and/or pimento slices. **Serves 8.**

Texas Quiche

1 tablespoon butter

$1/3$ cup sliced fresh mushrooms

2 small carrots, thinly sliced

10 eggs

$1/2$ teaspoon white pepper

$1/2$ teaspoon salt

1 teaspoon cumin

2 teaspoons sliced pickled jalapeño chiles with juice

$2^1/2$ cups evaporated milk

2 cups shredded Monterey Jack cheese

1 partially baked (10-inch) pie shell

$1/2$ cup canned green chiles, drained and sliced into thin strips

$2/3$ cup cubed cooked chicken

Additional strips green chiles (optional)

Melt the butter in a small skillet. Add the mushrooms and carrots and sauté until the vegetables are tender. Remove from the heat. Combine the eggs, white pepper, salt, cumin and jalapeños with juice in a blender. Process until well mixed. Add the evaporated milk and process until well mixed. Spread half the cheese in the pie shell. Spread the mushroom mixture over the cheese and top with $1/2$ cup green chiles and the chicken. Sprinkle with the remaining cheese. Pour the egg mixture over the cheese. Top with additional green chiles. Bake at 350 degrees for 1 hour and 45 minutes or until a knife inserted in the center comes out clean. Remove to a wire rack and let cool for at least 15 minutes. Cut into slices and garnish each slice with a dollop of sour cream and sliced black olives. **Serves 9 to 10.**

Vegetable Brunch Frittata

3 tablespoons olive oil

1 large onion, thinly sliced

3 garlic cloves, minced

3 summer squash, sliced 1/4 inch thick

3 zucchini, sliced 1/4 inch thick

1 red bell pepper, cut into 1/4-inch strips

1 yellow bell pepper, cut into 1/4-inch strips

1 green bell pepper, cut into 1/4-inch strips

8 ounces fresh mushrooms, sliced

6 eggs

1/4 cup heavy cream or half-and-half

2 teaspoons salt

2 teaspoons freshly ground pepper

2 cups (1/2-inch cubes) stale French bread

8 ounces cream cheese, cut into small pieces

2 cups shredded Swiss cheese

Heat the olive oil in a large saucepan. Add the onion, garlic, summer squash, zucchini, red bell pepper, yellow bell pepper, green bell pepper and mushrooms. Sauté for 15 minutes or until the vegetables are tender-crisp. Remove from the heat. Whisk the eggs, cream, salt and pepper in a large bowl. Stir in the bread, cream cheese and Swiss cheese. Add the sautéed vegetables and stir to mix well. Pour into a greased 10-inch springform pan and press down to pack tightly. Place on a foil-lined baking sheet. Bake at 350 degrees for 1 hour or until puffed, golden brown and firm to the touch. Cover the top of the frittata with foil while baking if becoming too brown. Remove to a wire rack. Loosen from the side of the pan with a sharp knife and remove the side. Serve hot, cold or at room temperature. **Serves 8.**

Shrimp and Grits

  4 cups water
  1 teaspoon salt
  1 cup grits
  $^1/_2$ cup (1 stick) butter
  2 cups shredded Cheddar cheese
  $^1/_4$ teaspoon garlic powder
  3 eggs
  $^3/_4$ cup half-and-half
  Shrimp (below)
  2 slices bacon, crisp-cooked and crumbled, or chopped ham
  Finely chopped fresh parsley

Bring the water and salt to a boil in a saucepan. Stir in the grits gradually. Cook for
5 minutes, stirring constantly. Remove from the heat and stir in the butter, cheese and
garlic powder. Beat the eggs and half-and-half in a bowl. Stir into the grits. Pour into
a greased 2-quart baking dish. Bake at 350 degrees for 45 minutes. Serve topped with
the Shrimp and sprinkled with the bacon and parsley. Garnish with lemon wedges.
Serves 4.

Shrimp

  1 tablespoon butter
  $^1/_4$ cup chopped onion
  21 to 26 deveined peeled fresh shrimp
  $1^1/_2$ teaspoons herbes de Provence
  $1^1/_2$ teaspoons Cajun seasoning
  1 tablespoon butter

Melt 1 tablespoon butter in a saucepan. Add the onion and sauté until tender. Add the
shrimp, herbes de Provence, Cajun seasoning and 1 tablespoon butter. Sauté until the
shrimp turn pink and a sauce forms.

Awesome Layered Grits

4 cups water

1 cup grits

1 teaspoon salt

1 (6-ounce) roll garlic cheese, chopped

$^1/_2$ cup (1 stick) butter

2 eggs, lightly beaten

$^1/_4$ cup milk

2 to 3 tomatoes, sliced

1 cup chopped fresh basil

1 large sweet onion, finely chopped

2 cups shredded Monterey Jack cheese

2 cups shredded Cheddar cheese

Bring the water to a boil in a saucepan. Stir in the grits and salt. Reduce the heat and cover. Simmer for 20 minutes or until thick. Remove from the heat and stir in the garlic cheese, butter, eggs and milk. Pour into a $2^1/_2$-quart baking dish. Bake at 350 degrees for 45 to 50 minutes. Remove to a wire rack and let cool. (May be made ahead up to this point and refrigerated.) Arrange the tomato slices on the grits. Sprinkle with the basil, onion, Monterey Jack cheese and Cheddar cheese. Bake at 350 degrees for 20 minutes or until hot. Cut into squares. **Serves 8 to 10.**

Savory Apple Baked Oatmeal

$1/2$ cup vegetable oil

$1/2$ cup sugar

2 eggs

3 cups quick-cooking oats

2 teaspoons baking powder

$1/2$ teaspoon salt

$1/2$ teaspoon cinnamon

1 cup milk

1 apple, peeled, cored and chopped

1 cup raisins

$1/4$ cup flaked coconut

1 cup sweetened dried cranberries

Beat the oil, sugar and eggs in a bowl until thick and pale yellow. Add the oats, baking powder, salt, cinnamon and milk and beat to mix well. Stir in the apple, raisins, coconut and cranberries. Pour into a greased 8×8-inch baking dish. Bake at 400 degrees for 30 to 40 minutes. Serve warm in bowls (the mixture will be crumbly) and top with brown sugar, milk or cream, or fresh fruit. **Serves 4 to 9.**

Note: This can be cut into 9 squares and frozen for individual portions.

Strawberries with Amaretto Yogurt

3 cups halved strawberries
2 tablespoons sugar or equivalent Splenda sweetener
1 (8-ounce) carton low-fat vanilla yogurt
2 tablespoons amaretto
Sliced almonds

Mix the strawberries and sugar in a bowl. Let stand for 5 to 10 minutes. Mix the yogurt and liqueur in a small bowl. Spoon the strawberries into serving bowls. Top with the yogurt mixture and sprinkle with almonds. **Serves 6.**

Hot Fruit Compote

12 coconut macaroon cookies, crumbled

4 (16-ounce) cans fruit, such as peaches, pears, apricots,
pineapple chunks or fruit cocktail, drained

^{1}/$_2$ cup chopped pecans

^{1}/$_4$ cup packed brown sugar

^{1}/$_2$ cup sherry (optional)

^{1}/$_4$ cup (^{1}/$_2$ stick) butter, melted

Spread half the crumbled cookies in a buttered 2^1/$_2$-quart baking dish. Mix the fruit
together in a bowl. Spread over the cookie layer. Top with the remaining crumbled
cookies. Sprinkle with the pecans, brown sugar and sherry. Bake at 350 degrees for
30 minutes. Drizzle with the melted butter. **Serves 16.**

Hot Fruit Salad

1 (15^1/4-ounce) can apricot halves
1 (14^1/2-ounce) can pear halves
1 (20-ounce) can pineapple chunks
3 large bananas, sliced
1 (15-ounce) can wild blueberries
1 (16-ounce) jar applesauce
1 (16-ounce) can cranberry sauce
Butter
Brown sugar

Drain the apricots, pears and pineapple in a colander. Top with the bananas and drain the blueberries over all. Combine the applesauce and cranberry sauce in a bowl. Stir to mix well. Spread half the applesauce mixture in a baking dish. Top with the well-drained fruit. Pour the remaining applesauce mixture over the fruit. Dot with butter and sprinkle with brown sugar. Bake at 350 degrees for 45 minutes or until the fruit is bubbly. Serve hot. **Serves 24.**

Caramel Pecan French Toast

1 cup packed brown sugar

$1/2$ cup (1 stick) butter

2 tablespoons light corn syrup

12 slices honey white bread

$3/4$ cup raisins

$3/4$ cup chopped pecans, toasted

6 eggs

1 cup heavy whipping cream

$1/2$ cup milk

2 teaspoons grated lemon zest

1 teaspoon vanilla extract

$1/2$ teaspoon cinnamon

$1/2$ cup heavy whipping cream

$1/4$ cup confectioners' sugar

Maple syrup

$1/4$ cup chopped pecans, toasted

Combine the brown sugar, butter and corn syrup in a small saucepan. Cook for 3 to 5 minutes or until the sugar dissolves, stirring constantly. Pour evenly into an ungreased 9×13-inch baking dish. Fit $1/2$ of the bread slices on top of the brown sugar mixture, cutting the bread if necessary to fit. Sprinkle with the raisins and $3/4$ cup pecans. Top with the remaining bread slices. Whisk the eggs, 1 cup cream, milk, lemon zest, vanilla, and cinnamon in a bowl. Pour over the bread slices. Bake at 350 degrees for 40 minutes or until a wooden pick inserted in the center comes out clean. Remove to a wire rack. Beat $1/2$ cup cream in a bowl until foamy. Beat in the confectioners' sugar gradually and beat until soft peaks form. Divide the French Toast among 8 serving plates. Top with the whipped cream and drizzle with maple syrup. Sprinkle with $1/4$ cup pecans. **Serves 8.**

Baked French Toast

1 loaf French bread, cut into 8 (1-inch) slices
6 eggs
3/4 cup milk
1/4 teaspoon baking powder
1 tablespoon vanilla extract
1 (10-ounce) package frozen strawberries, thawed
4 bananas, thickly sliced
3/4 cup sugar
1 tablespoon apple pie spice
Cinnamon-sugar
Whipped cream or confectioners' sugar

Fit the bread slices into a shallow baking dish. Beat the eggs, milk, baking powder and vanilla in a bowl. Pour over the bread. Cover and chill overnight. Mix the strawberries and bananas in a bowl. Spread in a 9×13-inch baking dish. Sprinkle with the sugar and apple pie spice. Place the soaked bread slices on top. Sprinkle with cinnamon-sugar. Bake at 450 degrees for 20 to 25 minutes. Serve topped with whipped cream or confectioners' sugar. **Serves 8.**

Sopapilla Cheesecake

2 (8-ounce) cans refrigerator
   crescent rolls
16 ounces cream cheese, softened
1 cup sugar

1 teaspoon vanilla extract
$^1/_2$ cup (1 stick) butter
1 cup sugar
1 teaspoon cinnamon

Unroll 1 can of the crescent dough and fit onto the bottom of a 9×13-inch baking pan coated with nonstick cooking spray. Press the seams to seal. Beat the cream cheese, 1 cup sugar and the vanilla in a bowl. Spread over the dough in the pan. Unroll the remaining can of crescent dough and press the seams to seal. Place on top of the cream cheese mixture. Melt the butter in a saucepan. Stir in 1 cup sugar and the cinnamon. Pour over the dough. Bake at 350 degrees for 30 to 35 minutes or until golden brown. **Serves 10 to 12.**

Fresh Rome Apple Cake

$1^1/_2$ cups corn oil
2 cups sugar
3 eggs
3 cups all-purpose flour
1 teaspoon baking powder
$^1/_2$ teaspoon baking soda

1 teaspoon salt
1 teaspoon cinnamon
1 teaspoon nutmeg
1 teaspoon vanilla extract
3 Rome apples, cored and grated
1 cup chopped nuts

Beat the oil, sugar and eggs in a large bowl. Mix the flour, baking powder, baking soda, salt, cinnamon and nutmeg together. Add to the egg mixture and stir to mix well. Stir in the vanilla, apples and nuts. Pour into a nonstick bundt or tube pan. Bake at 325 degrees for $1^1/_2$ hours or until a wooden pick inserted in the center comes out clean. Remove to a wire rack to cool. Serve with hot coffee. **Serves 12.**

Peaches and Cream Coffee Cake

$^3/_4$ cup all-purpose flour

1 teaspoon baking powder

$^1/_2$ teaspoon salt

1 (3-ounce) package vanilla pudding mix (not instant)

3 tablespoons butter, softened

1 egg

$^1/_2$ cup milk

1 (15-ounce) can sliced peaches, drained and
   $4^1/_2$ teaspoons juice reserved

4 ounces cream cheese, softened

$^1/_4$ cup sugar

1 tablespoon sugar

$^1/_2$ teaspoon cinnamon

$^1/_2$ cup fresh blueberries (optional)

Mix the flour, baking powder, salt and pudding mix in a bowl. Add the butter, egg
and milk. Beat for 2 minutes with an electric mixer at medium speed until well blended.
Pour into a greased pie plate. Arrange the peach slices on top in a spiral pattern.
Combine the cream cheese, reserved peach juice and $^1/_4$ cup sugar in a bowl. Beat
with an electric mixer at medium speed for 2 minutes. Spread over the batter to
within 1 inch of the edge. Mix 1 tablespoon sugar and the cinnamon in a small
bowl and sprinkle over the cream cheese mixture. Sprinkle with the blueberries. Bake
at 350 degrees for 30 to 35 minutes. Remove to a wire rack and let cool for at least
15 minutes. **Serves 6 to 8.**

Pecan Pie Muffins

1 cup packed brown sugar
$^1/_2$ cup sifted all-purpose flour
1 cup chopped pecans
$^1/_2$ cup (1 stick) plus $2^1/_2$ tablespoons butter, melted
2 eggs, beaten
$^3/_4$ teaspoon vanilla extract

Mix the brown sugar, flour and pecans in a bowl. Mix the melted butter, eggs and vanilla in a bowl. Add to the dry ingredients and stir to mix well. Fill greased muffin cups $^3/_4$ full. Bake at 350 degrees for 20 to 25 minutes or until a wooden pick inserted in the center comes out clean. Cool in the pans for 5 minutes. Remove to a wire rack to cool. **Makes 1 dozen muffins.**

Pumpkin Muffins

$^1/_2$ cup (1 stick) margarine, softened
1 cup packed brown sugar
1 egg
1 cup canned pumpkin
1$^1/_2$ cups all-purpose flour
1 teaspoon baking powder

1 teaspoon baking soda
1 cup dates, chopped
1 cup pecans, chopped
$^1/_2$ cup all-purpose flour
Orange Icing (below)

Beat the margarine and brown sugar in a large bowl until light and fluffy. Beat in the egg and pumpkin. Mix 1$^1/_2$ cups flour, the baking powder and baking soda together. Stir into the pumpkin mixture. Dredge the dates and pecans in $^1/_2$ cup flour. Stir into the pumpkin mixture. Fill greased and floured muffin cups. Bake at 375 degrees for 15 to 20 minutes for regular-size muffins or 10 minutes for mini-muffins or until a wooden pick inserted in the center comes out clean. Cool in the pans for 5 minutes. Remove to a wire rack. Frost with the Orange Icing while still warm. **Makes 2 dozen regular-size muffins or 4 dozen mini-muffins.**

Orange Icing

2 cups confectioners' sugar
3 ounces cream cheese, softened

Grated zest of 1 orange
1 to 2 teaspoons orange juice

Beat the confectioners' sugar, cream cheese, orange zest and orange juice in a bowl until smooth.

Blueberry Scones with Lemon Glaze

2 cups all-purpose flour
1 tablespoon baking powder
$1/2$ teaspoon salt
2 tablespoons sugar
5 tablespoons cold unsalted butter, cut into pieces
1 cup heavy cream
1 cup fresh blueberries
All-purpose flour
Lemon Glaze (below)

Sift 2 cups flour, baking powder, salt and sugar into a bowl. Cut in the butter with a pastry blender or fork until the consistency of coarse crumbs. Make a well in the center and fold in the cream. Stir just until blended. Dredge the blueberries in flour. Fold the blueberries gently into the dough. Pat the dough out on a lightly floured work surface to make a rectangle. Cut into four 3-inch squares. Cut each square diagonally to make 8 triangles. Place the scones on a parchment-lined baking sheet. Bake at 400 degrees for 15 to 20 minutes or until golden brown. Remove the scones to a wire rack to cool. Drizzle the Lemon Glaze on the cooled scones and let stand for a few minutes. **Serves 8.**

Lemon Glaze

$1/2$ cup freshly squeezed lemon juice
2 cups confectioners' sugar, sifted
Grated zest of 1 lemon
1 tablespoon unsalted butter

Combine the lemon juice and confectioners' sugar in a microwave-safe bowl. Stir until the sugar dissolves. Stir in the lemon zest and butter. Microwave on High for 30 seconds. Whisk until smooth.

Sweet Potato Biscuits

3 envelopes dry yeast
$3/4$ cup warm water
$7^1/2$ cups all-purpose flour
1 tablespoon baking powder
1 tablespoon salt
$1^1/2$ cups sugar
$1^1/2$ cups shortening
3 cups mashed cooked sweet potatoes

Stir the yeast and warm water in a 2-cup measuring cup. Let stand for 5 minutes. Mix the flour, baking powder, salt and sugar in a large bowl. Cut in the shortening with a pastry blender or fork until crumbly. Add the yeast mixture and sweet potatoes and stir just until blended. Turn out the dough onto a lightly floured work surface. Knead for 5 minutes or until smooth and elastic. Place in a well-greased bowl, turning to grease all sides of the dough. Cover and chill for 8 hours, if desired. Roll out the dough on a floured work surface to $1/2$ inch thick. Cut with a 2-inch biscuit cutter. Wrap and freeze for up to 1 month, if desired. Place the biscuits on an ungreased baking sheet. Cover and let rise in a warm place for 20 minutes or until doubled in bulk. Bake at 400 degrees for 10 to 12 minutes or until light brown. **Makes $7^1/2$ dozen biscuits.**

Note: Increase the rising time if the biscuits were frozen.

Easter Resurrection Rolls

1 (8-ounce) can refrigerator crescent rolls
8 large marshmallows
1/2 cup (1 stick) butter, melted
Cinnamon-sugar

Separate the crescent rolls on a work surface and flatten. Wrap each marshmallow in a crescent roll. Dip the top of each roll in the melted butter and then in cinnamon-sugar. Place the rolls in greased muffin cups, sugar side up. Bake at 350 degrees for 10 minutes. Remove to a wire rack to cool. **Serves 8.**

Note: "These Easter treats are special as the name implies, because just like the Tomb, they are empty inside!"

Poppy Seed Bread

3 cups all-purpose flour

$1^1/2$ teaspoons baking powder

$1^1/2$ cups milk

$1^1/2$ teaspoons vanilla extract

$1^1/2$ teaspoons almond extract

$1^1/2$ teaspoons butter flavoring

$4^1/2$ teaspoons poppy seeds

$2^1/2$ cups sugar

3 eggs

1 cup plus 2 tablespoons vegetable oil

Glaze (below)

Combine the flour, baking powder, milk, vanilla, almond extract, butter flavoring, poppy seeds, sugar, eggs and oil in a large bowl. Beat with an electric mixer for 2 minutes. Pour into 2 lightly greased 4×8-inch loaf pans. Bake at 350 degrees for $1^1/4$ hours or until a wooden pick inserted in the center comes out clean. Cool in the pans for 10 minutes. Remove to a wire rack to cool completely. Pour the Glaze over the cooled loaves. **Serves 24.**

Note: This bread freezes well.

Glaze

$1/2$ teaspoon vanilla extract

$1/2$ teaspoon almond extract

$1/2$ teaspoon butter flavoring

$1/4$ cup orange juice

$3/4$ cup confectioners' sugar

Combine the vanilla, almond extract, butter flavoring, orange juice and confectioners' sugar in a bowl. Beat until smooth.

Strawberry Bread

3 cups all-purpose flour
1 teaspoon baking soda
1 teaspoon salt
1 tablespoon cinnamon
2 cups sugar
4 eggs, beaten
2 cups frozen strawberries in syrup, thawed
1 1/2 cups vegetable oil
1 1/4 cups chopped pecans

Sift the flour, baking soda, salt, cinnamon and sugar into a large bowl. Mix the eggs, strawberries and oil in a bowl. Add to the dry ingredients and stir to mix. Stir in the pecans. Pour into 2 greased and floured 4×8-inch loaf pans. Bake at 325 degrees for 45 minutes to 1 hour or until a wooden pick inserted in the center comes out clean. Cool in the pans for 10 minutes. Remove to a wire rack to cool completely. **Serves 24.**

Note: This bread freezes well.

Focaccia Topped with Sun-Dried Tomatoes, Basil and Goat Cheese

8 sun-dried tomatoes

1 (10-ounce) package Afghan bread, sliced

1¹/2 teaspoons garlic-infused olive oil

2 ounces goat cheese, crumbled

1/4 cup coarsely chopped fresh basil

Grated Parmesan cheese (optional)

Cover the tomatoes with boiling water in a bowl. Let stand for 30 minutes. Drain and chop. Brush the bread lightly with the olive oil. Spread the tomatoes over the bread. Sprinkle with the goat cheese, basil and Parmesan cheese. Place on a baking sheet. Bake at 350 degrees for 5 minutes or until the cheese melts and the top is crisp. **Serves 12.**

Note: Afghan bread is found in the bakery section at your local grocery store. Focaccia bread may be used if Afghan bread is not available.

Broccoli Jalapeño Corn Bread

1 (10-ounce) package frozen chopped broccoli

4 eggs, lightly beaten

1 (12-ounce) carton cottage cheese

1 to 2 jalapeño chiles, seeded and finely chopped

1/2 cup finely chopped onion

3/4 cup (1¹/2 sticks) butter, melted

2 (8¹/2-ounce) packages corn bread mix

Cook the broccoli in a saucepan of boiling water for 6 minutes; drain. Combine the eggs, cottage cheese, jalapeños, onion and melted butter in a large bowl. Stir to mix well. Stir in the corn bread mix and broccoli. Pour into a greased 9×13-inch baking pan. Bake at 350 degrees for 30 to 35 minutes or until a wooden pick inserted in the center comes out clean. Remove to a wire rack to cool. **Serves 18.**

"*The pleasures of the table are a natural accompaniment to the pleasures of life.*"

—Julia Child

Sumptuous
Soups & Salads

Hunter's Stew

6 thick slices bacon

3 pounds beef stew meat

1 pound boneless pork, cut into
  1 1/2-inch pieces

3 (16-ounce) cans tomatoes

1 (10 ounce) can tomatoes with
  green chiles

3 celery ribs, sliced

6 onions, chopped

6 garlic cloves, minced

1/2 cup Worcestershire sauce

2 tablespoons chili powder

2 cups water

Salt to taste

Sugar to taste

8 small potatoes, cut into 1/2-inch
  pieces

1 pound carrots, sliced diagonally
  into 1 1/2-inch pieces

1 (16-ounce) can green peas

1 (16-ounce) can cut green beans

1 (16-ounce) can whole kernel corn

1 (16-ounce) can cut okra (optional)

Cook the bacon in a large cast-iron stockpot until crisp. Remove to paper towels to drain; crumble. Add the beef and pork to the bacon drippings. Brown quickly in the hot fat. Reduce the heat and stir in the tomatoes, tomatoes with green chiles, celery, onions, garlic, Worcestershire sauce, chili powder and water. Season with salt. Cover and cook over very low heat for 2 hours or until the meat is tender. Season with sugar. Stir in the potatoes and carrots. Cover and cook until the vegetables are tender. Stir in the peas, green beans, corn, okra and cooked bacon. Cover and cook for 10 minutes.
Serves 10 to 12.

Burgundy Beef Stew

2 pounds beef stew meat
All-purpose flour for dredging
4 slices bacon
2 onions, chopped
1 to 2 cups red wine
3 bay leaves
4 to 6 whole cloves
2 beef bouillon cubes
1 cup water
4 carrots, diced
8 ounces fresh mushroom caps

Dredge the beef in flour. Cook the bacon in a large heavy saucepan until crisp. Add the beef and sauté until brown. Stir in the onions, wine, bay leaves, cloves, bouillon cubes and water. Cook, covered, over low heat for 1 hour. Stir in the carrots. Cook, covered, for 50 minutes. Stir in the mushrooms and cook for 10 minutes. Remove and discard the bay leaves and whole cloves. Serve with a green salad, crusty bread and a glass of red wine on a cool fall or winter evening. **Serves 4 to 6.**

Taco Stew

1¹/2 pounds ground beef
1 small onion, chopped
1 envelope taco seasoning mix
1 (1-ounce) package ranch salad
    dressing mix
6 ounces small shell pasta, cooked al
    dente and drained
1 (15-ounce) can ranch-style beans

1 (16-ounce) can black-eyed peas with
    jalapeños
1 (14³/4-ounce) can cream-style corn
1 (15¹/2-ounce) can hominy
1 (10-ounce) can tomatoes with
    green chiles
2 cups water

Brown the ground beef in a large saucepan with the onion, stirring until the ground beef is crumbly; drain. Stir in the taco seasoning mix, salad dressing mix, pasta, beans, black-eyed peas, corn, hominy, tomatoes with green chiles and water. Simmer for 30 minutes. **Serves 12.**

Posole, Santa Fe-Style

1 large onion, chopped
2 garlic cloves, minced
2 pounds lean pork spareribs
2 quarts water
3 cans golden hominy, rinsed and
    drained

2 tablespoons chili powder
1 teaspoon oregano
1 teaspoon cumin
Salt and pepper to taste
Tabasco sauce to taste

Combine the onion, garlic, pork and water in a large saucepan. Cook over low heat for 2 hours or until the meat falls off the bones. Remove the meat from the bones and discard the bones and any visible fat. Return the meat to the saucepan. Stir in the hominy, chili powder, oregano and cumin. Season with salt and pepper. Simmer, uncovered, for 15 to 30 minutes. Season with Tabasco sauce and add more cumin, if desired. Serve with hot corn bread on a cold day. **Serves 6.**

Mexican Chicken Corn Chowder

3 tablespoons butter or margarine

4 boneless skinless chicken breasts, cut into
   bite-size pieces (about 1^1/$_2$ pounds)

1 small onion, chopped

3 garlic cloves, chopped

2 cups half-and-half

2 cups shredded Monterey Jack cheese

2 (14^3/$_4$-ounce) cans cream-style corn

1 (4^1/$_2$-ounce) can chopped green chiles

^{1}/$_2$ teaspoon Tabasco sauce

^{1}/$_2$ to 1 teaspoon cumin

^{1}/$_4$ teaspoon salt

2 tablespoons chopped fresh cilantro (optional)

Melt the butter in a large heavy saucepan over medium-high heat. Add the chicken, onion and garlic and sauté for 10 minutes. Reduce the heat to low and stir in the half-and-half, cheese, corn, green chiles, Tabasco sauce, cumin and salt. Cook for 15 minutes, stirring often. Stir in the cilantro. Spoon into serving bowls and garnish with chopped Anaheim chile and chopped cilantro. **Serves 8.**

Shrimp and Corn Chowder

1 tablespoon butter

$^1/_4$ cup chopped green onions

1 garlic clove, minced

$1^1/_8$ teaspoons garlic pepper

2 ($10^3/_4$-ounce) cans condensed cream of potato soup

3 ounces cream cheese, softened

2 cups milk

$^1/_8$ teaspoon cayenne pepper

2 cups frozen deveined peeled shrimp

1 (8-ounce) can whole kernel corn

Melt the butter in a saucepan. Add the green onions, garlic and garlic pepper and sauté until the vegetables are tender. Stir in the soup, cream cheese, milk and cayenne pepper. Stir in the shrimp and corn. Bring to a boil and reduce the heat. Simmer, covered, for 10 minutes or until the shrimp turn pink. **Serves 8.**

Chicken Tortilla Soup

$1/2$ teaspoon olive oil

2 boneless skinless chicken breasts, cut into bite-size pieces (about $2/3$ pound)

1 cup chopped onion

1 tablespoon lime juice

$1/2$ teaspoon minced garlic

$1/2$ teaspoon chili powder

$1/4$ teaspoon cumin

2 ($14^1/2$-ounce) cans fat-free chicken broth

1 cup salsa

1 cup corn kernels (optional)

$2^1/2$ cups crushed tortilla chips

$1/4$ cup shredded Monterey Jack cheese

Heat the olive oil in a $4^1/2$-quart heavy saucepan over low heat. Increase the heat to high and add the chicken. Sauté for 2 minutes. Add the onion, lime juice, garlic, chili powder and cumin and sauté for 2 minutes. Stir in the chicken broth, salsa and corn. Cover and bring to a boil. Reduce the heat to medium-high and boil for 8 to 10 minutes. Divide the tortilla chips among 6 serving bowls. Ladle the soup over the chips and sprinkle with the cheese. **Serves 6.**

Artichoke Soup

1 (10³/4-ounce) can condensed cream
   of celery soup
1¹/3 cups milk
¹/2 cup shredded sharp Cheddar cheese
3 tablespoons sherry

1 small can artichoke hearts, drained,
   or 1 package frozen artichoke hearts,
   thawed
Tabasco sauce (optional)
Grated onion (optional)

Mix the soup, milk, cheese, sherry and artichokes in a saucepan. Cook until heated through, stirring occasionally. Serve with Tabasco sauce and/or grated onion.
Serves 2 to 4.

Cream of Mushroom Soup

¹/4 cup (¹/2 stick) butter
³/4 cup chopped green onions (white
   and green parts)
2 cups chopped fresh mushrooms
2 tablespoons all-purpose flour

1 cup chicken broth
1 cup half-and-half
¹/4 teaspoon salt
¹/4 teaspoon pepper

Melt the butter in a skillet over low heat. Add the green onions and sauté for 5 minutes or until tender. Add the mushrooms and sauté for 2 minutes. Add the flour and cook for 3 minutes, stirring constantly. Remove from the heat and whisk in the chicken broth and half-and-half in a steady stream. Bring to a boil over medium heat. Simmer for 5 minutes. Stir in the salt and pepper. **Serves 4 to 6.**

Note: This soup is best made ahead and reheated when ready to serve.

Loaded Potato Soup

6 cups water

2 chicken bouillon cubes

1 (2-pound) bag frozen hash brown potatoes

2 tablespoons finely chopped onion

1 teaspoon chopped parsley

1 teaspoon chopped chives

1/2 teaspoon basil

1/4 teaspoon garlic powder

Salt and pepper to taste

2 cups milk

16 ounces Velveeta cheese, cubed

8 ounces bacon, crisp-cooked and crumbled

Bring the water to a boil in large saucepan. Add the bouillon cubes and cook until the bouillon dissolves. Stir in the potatoes, onion, parsley, chives, basil and garlic powder. Season with salt and pepper. Bring to a boil and reduce the heat. Cook for 10 minutes or until the potatoes are tender. Remove from the heat and stir in the milk slowly. Add the cheese. Cook over low heat until the cheese melts, stirring constantly. Ladle into serving bowls and top with the bacon. **Serves 6.**

Perfect Pumpkin Soup

$1/4$ cup ($1/2$ stick) butter
1 large onion, chopped
2 cups canned pumpkin
$2^{1}/2$ cups chicken broth
$1^{1}/2$ teaspoons salt
$1/2$ teaspoon curry powder
2 cups heavy cream
Chopped fresh parsley

Melt the butter in a heavy saucepan. Add the onion and sauté until tender. Stir in the pumpkin, chicken broth, salt and curry powder. Simmer for 45 minutes; do not let boil. Stir in the cream and ladle into serving bowls. Sprinkle with chopped parsley. **Serves 12.**

Brie Soup

¹/2 cup (1 stick) butter

1 pound carrots, peeled and chopped

1 pound celery, chopped

2 white onions, chopped

1 cup white wine

¹/4 teaspoon cracked black pepper

2¹/4 cups chicken stock

¹/4 to ¹/2 cup heavy cream

4 cups milk

¹/2 cup cornstarch

¹/2 cup soft Brie cheese, rind removed

1 bunch green onions, chopped (white and green parts)

4 ounces fresh mushrooms, thinly sliced

Melt the butter in a large saucepan. Add the carrots, celery and white onions. Sauté over medium-high heat for 5 minutes or until the onions are golden brown. Stir in the wine and pepper. Reduce the heat to low and simmer for 5 minutes. Stir in the chicken stock and increase the heat to high. Boil for 5 minutes. Remove from the heat and stir in the cream and milk. Whisk in the cornstarch gradually. Simmer over medium heat for 7 minutes or until thickened; do not let boil. Pour through a fine wire-mesh strainer or damp cheesecloth into a saucepan; discard the carrots, celery and white onions. Add the cheese and cook gently until the cheese melts. Stir in the green onions and mushrooms. Cook until heated through and serve immediately. **Serves 8.**

Beer Cheese Soup

2^1/2 cups milk

^{1}/2 cup processed cheese spread

2 tablespoons cornstarch

^{1}/2 cup cold water

1 teaspoon chicken bouillon granules

1 teaspoon Tabasco sauce

1 teaspoon Worcestershire sauce

^{1}/3 cup beer

Heat the milk in a heavy saucepan over low heat until warm. Add the cheese and cook until melted, whisking constantly. Mix the cornstarch and water in a small bowl. Stir into the cheese mixture. Cook until thickened, stirring constantly. Stir in the bouillon granules, Tabasco sauce and Worcestershire sauce. Pour the soup through a fine wire-mesh strainer or damp cheesecloth into a saucepan. Stir in the beer. Cook until heated through; do not let boil. Serve hot. **Serves 4.**

Mozzarella Chicken Salad

3 large boneless skinless chicken
   breasts
Minced garlic
Finely chopped onion
1 cup chopped celery
1/2 teaspoon salt
2 tablespoons chopped fresh parsley

1 cup chopped pecans or almonds
8 ounces mozzarella cheese, cubed
3 cups seedless grapes
1 cup mayonnaise
1/2 cup heavy whipping cream,
   whipped

Simmer the chicken, garlic and onion in a saucepan of boiling water until the chicken is cooked through. Remove the chicken and let cool. Shred the chicken and place in a large bowl. Stir in the celery, salt, parsley, pecans, cheese, grapes, mayonnaise and whipped cream. Chill until cold. **Serves 8.**

Waldorf Chicken Salad

5 chicken breasts, cooked, boned and
   cut into bite-size pieces
1 Red Delicious apple, cored and
   chopped
3 celery ribs, chopped
3/4 cup raisins

3/4 cup chopped pecans
1/3 cup finely chopped onion
3/4 to 1 cup mayonnaise
Salt and pepper to taste
Garlic salt to taste

Mix the chicken, apple, celery, raisins, pecans, onion and mayonnaise in a large bowl. Season with salt, pepper and garlic salt. Cover and chill. Serve on a bed of lettuce as a salad or on croissants for sandwiches. **Serves 8 to 10.**

Fiesta Chicken Salad with Lime-Cilantro Vinaigrette

1/2 cup chopped shallots

1/4 cup fresh lime juice

1/4 cup chopped fresh cilantro

1 tablespoon minced garlic

1/2 cup vegetable oil

Salt and pepper to taste

3 cups thinly sliced red leaf lettuce

3 cups thinly sliced napa cabbage

1 cup diced cooked chicken breast

2 plum tomatoes, seeded and chopped

1/2 red bell pepper, thinly sliced

1/2 yellow bell pepper, thinly sliced

1/2 avocado, diced

1/3 cup crumbled tortilla chips

1/4 cup cooked fresh corn kernels or frozen corn kernels, thawed

1/4 cup pumpkin seeds, toasted

1/4 cup thinly sliced red onion

1/2 cup crumbled queso anejo cheese or feta cheese

Mix the shallots, lime juice, cilantro and garlic in a bowl. Whisk in the oil gradually. Season with salt and pepper. Combine the lettuce, cabbage, chicken, tomatoes, red bell pepper, yellow bell pepper, avocado, tortilla chips, corn, pumpkin seeds and onion in a large bowl. Add the lime vinaigrette and toss to coat. Top with the cheese. **Serves 10 to 12.**

Note: The lime vinaigrette can be made 1 day ahead. Cover and chill. Bring to room temperature before using.

Curried Chicken Salad

2³/4 pounds boneless chicken breasts

Olive oil

Cracked pepper

Kosher salt

Thyme (optional)

1 (11-ounce) can mandarin oranges, drained well

2 cups seedless red grapes, halved

1 (8-ounce) can sliced water chestnuts, drained and chopped

1 cup thinly sliced celery

1/3 cup light mayonnaise

1/3 cup low-fat lemon yogurt

2 teaspoons soy sauce

1 teaspoon curry powder

Salt to taste

Rub the chicken with olive oil and sprinkle with pepper, kosher salt and thyme on both sides. Place in a shallow baking pan. Bake at 350 degrees for 20 minutes or until the chicken is cooked through. Remove the chicken to a work surface and let cool. Chop and place in a large bowl. Add the oranges, grapes, water chestnuts and celery. Toss gently to mix. Stir the mayonnaise, yogurt, soy sauce and curry powder in a small bowl. Season with salt. Add to the chicken mixture and toss gently to coat. Cover and chill for up to 24 hours. **Serves 8 to 10.**

Egg Salad

6 hard-cooked eggs, chopped

2 tablespoons sweet pickle relish

2 tablespoons chopped fresh parsley

1 tablespoon finely chopped yellow
onion

$^1/_2$ teaspoon dillweed

1 tablespoon juice from pickled
jalapeño chiles

$^1/_2$ teaspoon curry powder

$^1/_4$ teaspoon dry mustard

$^1/_4$ teaspoon pepper

6 tablespoons Herb Mayonnaise (below)

Combine the eggs, relish, parsley, onion, dillweed, jalapeño juice, curry powder, dry mustard, pepper and Herb Mayonnaise in a bowl. Stir gently to mix. **Serves 2 to 4.**

Herb Mayonnaise

$^1/_2$ cup fresh parsley sprigs

1 green onion

$^1/_4$ teaspoon minced garlic

3 eggs

1 tablespoon lemon juice

$1^1/_2$ teaspoons cider vinegar

$1^1/_2$ teaspoons whole grain mustard

$1^1/_2$ teaspoons dillweed

1 teaspoon salt

$^1/_2$ teaspoon white pepper

Dash of Tabasco sauce

$2^1/_4$ cups canola oil

Combine the parsley, green onion, garlic, eggs, lemon juice, vinegar, mustard, dillweed, salt, white pepper and Tabasco sauce in a food processor or blender. Process until finely chopped. Add the oil slowly with the machine running, processing until thickened. **Makes 4 cups.**

Note: If you are concerned about using raw eggs, use eggs pasteurized in their shells, available in some specialty food stores.

Wild Tuna Salad

1 (6-ounce) package long grain and wild rice

1 cup mayonnaise

$1/2$ cup sour cream

$1/2$ cup chopped celery

2 tablespoons chopped onion

$1/2$ teaspoon salt

$1/4$ teaspoon pepper

2 (7-ounce) cans solid white tuna, drained and flaked

1 cup cashews, toasted

Prepare the rice according to the package directions. Let stand until cool. Combine the rice, mayonnaise, sour cream, celery, onion, salt, pepper and tuna in a bowl. Stir to mix well. Cover and chill overnight. Top with the cashews just before serving. **Serves 6 to 8.**

Tunisian Eggplant Salad

1 cup water

2 pounds eggplant, cut into 1-inch cubes

2 large green bell peppers, chopped

2 garlic cloves, crushed

1 cup olive oil

$^2/3$ cup red wine vinegar

2 teaspoons oregano, crushed

2 teaspoons salt

2 (12$^1/2$-ounce) cans chunk-style tuna, drained

2 large tomatoes, seeded and chopped

Crisp salad greens

$^1/2$ cup crumbled feta cheese

Bring the water to a boil in a saucepan. Place the eggplant in a steamer basket. Steam over the boiling water for 2 to 5 minutes or until tender; drain. Arrange the eggplant and bell peppers in a shallow 2-quart baking dish. Combine the garlic, olive oil, vinegar, oregano and salt in a jar with a tight-fitting lid. Shake to mix well. Pour over the eggplant and bell peppers. Cover and chill for 1 hour. Drain the eggplant mixture. Add the tuna and tomatoes and toss to mix. Line a salad bowl with crisp greens. Fill with the tuna mixture and sprinkle with the feta cheese. **Serves 10 to 12.**

Caribbean Shrimp and Black Bean Salad

1 (15-ounce) can black beans, rinsed and drained

1 small green bell pepper, finely chopped

1/2 cup sliced celery

1/2 cup sliced purple onion, separated into rings

2 tablespoons chopped fresh cilantro

2/3 cup picante sauce

1/4 cup lime juice

2 tablespoons vegetable oil

2 tablespoons honey

1/4 teaspoon salt

3 cups water

2 pounds unpeeled fresh medium shrimp

Lettuce leaves

Cherry tomato halves

Combine the black beans, bell pepper, celery, onion, cilantro, picante sauce, lime juice, oil, honey and salt in a large bowl. Toss gently to mix. Cover and chill for 8 hours. Bring the water to a boil in a saucepan. Add the shrimp and cook for 3 minutes or until the shrimp turn pink; drain. Peel and devein the shrimp and let cool. Add to the bean mixture and toss to mix. Serve over lettuce leaves and top with cherry tomato halves.

Serves 4 to 6.

Orzo Shrimp Salad

1 pound orzo

2 teaspoons extra-virgin olive oil

1 pound small peeled cooked shrimp

1 cup frozen green peas

1/4 cup chopped fresh basil

3 ounces feta cheese, crumbled

4 ripe tomatoes, cored and chopped (about 1 pound)

2 tablespoons extra-virgin olive oil

1 tablespoon red wine vinegar

1 teaspoon fresh lemon juice

Salt and freshly ground pepper to taste

Salad greens

Chopped fresh basil (optional)

Cook the orzo in a large saucepan of boiling salted water until al dente. Drain and rinse thoroughly with cold water; drain again. Remove to a large bowl. Add 2 teaspoons olive oil and toss to coat. Add the shrimp, peas, 1/4 cup basil and cheese and toss to mix. Combine the tomatoes, 2 tablespoons olive oil, vinegar and lemon juice in a bowl. Season with salt and pepper. Stir to mix well. Add to the orzo mixture and toss to coat. Serve in a large bowl or individual serving plates lined with salad greens and top with additional chopped basil. **Serves 4 to 6.**

Note: This salad can be made a few hours ahead without the cheese and basil. Cover and chill. Bring to room temperature before adding the cheese and basil. Toss to mix and serve immediately.

Chicken and Artichoke Pasta Salad

1 pound orzo
1 tablespoon extra-virgin olive oil
1 boneless skinless chicken breast
14 to 16 ounces canned artichoke hearts or frozen artichoke hearts, thawed
Basil-Tomato Dressing (below)
Salt and freshly ground pepper to taste

Cook the orzo in a large saucepan of boiling salted water until al dente. Drain and rinse thoroughly with cold water; drain again. Remove to a large bowl. Add the olive oil and toss to coat. Poach the chicken in enough simmering water to cover in a saucepan for 15 minutes or until cooked through. Remove the chicken and cut into cubes. Add to the orzo. Rinse the artichokes and cut into quarters. Add to the orzo mixture. Add the Basil-Tomato Dressing and toss well to coat. Season with salt and pepper. Serve garnished with basil sprigs. **Serves 4 to 6.**

Basil-Tomato Dressing

3 large ripe tomatoes, cored and finely chopped
1/4 cup chopped fresh basil
1/2 cup chopped fresh parsley
3 garlic cloves, minced
3 tablespoons red wine vinegar
1 tablespoon extra-virgin olive oil
1/2 teaspoon salt
Freshly ground pepper to taste

Combine the tomatoes, basil, parsley, garlic, vinegar, olive oil and salt in a bowl. Season with pepper. Stir to mix well.

Greek Pasta Salad

10 ounces vermicelli, cooked al dente and drained

$^1/_4$ to $^1/_2$ cup extra-virgin olive oil

2 tablespoons (or more) Cavender's Greek Seasoning

3 tablespoons fresh lemon juice

1 ($2^1/_4$-ounce) can chopped black olives, drained

1 (2-ounce) jar pimentos, drained

$^1/_4$ cup mayonnaise

5 green onions, sliced (white and green parts)

Cut the cooked and cooled pasta into 3- to 4-inch pieces and place in a large bowl. Add the olive oil, Greek seasoning and lemon juice. Toss to coat. Add the olives, pimentos, mayonnaise and green onions and toss to mix. Cover and chill for at least 4 hours.
Serves 4.

Broccoli Salad

6 cups chopped broccoli florets

1 cup diced red onion

$1/2$ cup raisins or sweetened dried cranberries

$1/3$ cup sunflower seeds

6 slices bacon, crisp-cooked and crumbled

$1/2$ cup shredded Cheddar cheese or crumbled feta cheese

$3/4$ cup mayonnaise

$1/4$ cup sugar

2 tablespoons vinegar

Combine the broccoli, onion, raisins, sunflower seeds, bacon and cheese in a large bowl. Toss to mix. Combine the mayonnaise, sugar and vinegar in a small bowl. Stir to mix well. Add to the broccoli mixture and toss to coat. Cover and chill. **Serves 8 to 10.**

Cauliflower-Broccoli Salad

4 cups small cauliflower florets

3 cups small broccoli florets

4 green onions, thinly sliced

3/4 cup sliced radishes

1/2 cup shredded carrots

1/2 cup golden raisins

1 cup mayonnaise or salad dressing

2 tablespoons sugar or equivalent Splenda sweetener

1 tablespoon lemon juice

2 teaspoons horseradish

1/2 teaspoon salt

1/2 teaspoon pepper

6 slices bacon, crisp-cooked and crumbled

Layer the cauliflower, broccoli, green onions, radishes, carrots and raisins in a large bowl. Combine the mayonnaise, sugar, lemon juice, horseradish, salt and pepper in a bowl. Stir to mix well. Spread over the vegetables and sprinkle with the bacon. Cover and chill for at least 4 hours and up to 24 hours. Stir to mix before serving. **Serves 8 to 10.**

Chinese Slaw

1 bag broccoli slaw mix
1 head cabbage, cored and shredded
1 small green bell pepper, finely chopped
8 green onions, finely chopped
$1/3$ cup red wine vinegar
$2/3$ cup sugar
1 teaspoon salt
1 teaspoon pepper
1 cup vegetable oil
$1/2$ cup (1 stick) butter
$3/4$ cup slivered almonds
1 bottle sesame seeds
2 (3-ounce) packages chicken-flavor ramen noodles, broken into pieces

Combine the broccoli slaw, cabbage, bell pepper and green onions in a large bowl. Toss to mix. Whisk the vinegar, sugar, salt, pepper and oil in a bowl. Cover and chill. Melt the butter in a skillet. Add the almonds, sesame seeds, noodles and seasoning packets. Sauté until golden brown. Remove from the heat. Add to the cabbage mixture and toss to mix. Add the dressing and toss to coat. Cover and chill for 1 hour. **Serves 10 to 12.**

Corn Bread Salad

1 (1-ounce) package ranch salad dressing mix

1 cup sour cream

1 cup mayonnaise

3 large tomatoes, cored and chopped

$1/2$ cup chopped green bell pepper

$1/2$ cup chopped red bell pepper

$1/2$ cup chopped green onions

1 (8-ounce) package corn bread mix, prepared according
to the package directions and cooled

2 (16-ounce) cans pinto beans, drained

2 cups shredded Cheddar cheese

10 slices bacon, crisp-cooked and crumbled

2 ($15^1/4$-ounce) cans whole kernel corn, drained

Combine the salad dressing mix, sour cream and mayonnaise in a bowl. Stir to mix well. Combine the tomatoes, green bell pepper, red bell pepper and green onions in a bowl. Toss gently to mix. Crumble half the corn bread into a 3-quart trifle bowl or large salad bowl. Top with $1/2$ of the tomato mixture, $1/2$ of the beans, $1/2$ of the cheese, $1/2$ of the bacon, $1/2$ of the corn and $1/2$ of the sour cream mixture. Repeat the layers. Cover and chill for at least 3 hours and up to 24 hours. **Serves 12 to 16.**

Lentil and Walnut Salad

3 cloves
1 onion, peeled
2 cups red lentils
3 carrots, halved
4 cups chicken stock
1 bay leaf
1 teaspoon thyme
$1/4$ cup white vinegar
$1/4$ cup vegetable oil
Salt and freshly ground pepper to taste
1 cup thinly sliced leeks or green onions
$1/2$ cup walnut or pecan halves
Chopped fresh parsley for garnish

Insert the cloves into the onion and place in a large saucepan. Add the lentils, carrots, chicken stock, bay leaf and thyme. Bring to a boil over medium heat. Reduce the heat and skim off any foam. Simmer for 15 minutes or until the lentils are tender but still retain their shape; do not overcook. Drain and discard the onion with cloves, carrots and bay leaf. Place the lentils in a bowl. Whisk the vinegar and oil in a small bowl. Pour over the hot lentils. Toss gently to coat. Season with salt and pepper. Let cool to room temperature. Toss gently to mix. Cover and chill overnight. Add the leeks and walnuts and toss gently to mix. Sprinkle with chopped parsley. **Serves 8.**

German Potato Salad

5 pounds unpeeled potatoes, scrubbed

Salt

2 cups finely chopped onions

2 cups canned chicken stock

$2/3$ cup olive oil

2 tablespoons white wine vinegar

4 teaspoons Dijon mustard

$2^1/2$ teaspoons salt, or to taste

2 teaspoons freshly ground pepper

2 tablespoons lemon juice

Boil the potatoes in a large saucepan of lightly salted water until tender; do not overcook. Drain and cut into $1/4$-inch slices. Place the hot potatoes in a large bowl and cover with foil. Combine the onions, chicken stock, olive oil, vinegar, mustard, salt and pepper in a saucepan. Bring to a boil and boil for 5 minutes. Remove from the heat and stir in the lemon juice. Pour over the potatoes and stir gently with a rubber spatula to coat. Cover and chill for 24 hours. Let stand at room temperature for 1 hour before serving. **Serves 12 to 14.**

Autumn Spinach Salad

1 large bag baby spinach

3/4 cup dry-roasted peanuts

3 to 4 green onions, chopped

2 Red Delicious apples, cored and chopped

3/4 cup raisins, golden raisins or sweetened dried cranberries

Freshly ground pepper

1/2 cup white wine vinegar

1/2 cup vegetable oil

1 teaspoon dry mustard

1 teaspoon curry powder

1/4 cup chutney

Place the spinach in a large salad bowl. Sprinkle with the peanuts and green onions. Top with the apples and raisins. Season with pepper. Whisk the vinegar, oil, dry mustard, curry powder and chutney in a bowl. Pour evenly over the salad. **Serves 8.**

Spinach Salad with Raspberry Vinaigrette

1 bag spinach
1 (11-ounce) can mandarin oranges, drained
1 avocado, pitted and sliced
1 red onion, sliced into rings
6 to 7 slices bacon, crisp-cooked and crumbled
1 cup seedless red grapes, halved or quartered
1 cup cashews
Raspberry Vinaigrette (below)

Combine the spinach, oranges, avocado, onion, bacon and grapes in a large salad bowl. Toss gently to mix. Add the cashews and Raspberry Vinaigrette and toss gently to coat. **Serves 6.**

Raspberry Vinaigrette

2 cups canola oil
3/4 cup raspberry vinegar
1/4 cup sugar
2 tablespoons lemon juice
1 tablespoon honey
2 teaspoons salt
1 teaspoon dry mustard
2 tablespoons poppy seeds

Whisk the oil, vinegar, sugar, lemon juice, honey, salt and dry mustard in a bowl. Whisk in the poppy seeds.

Dallas Spinach Salad

1 (10-ounce) bag baby spinach
1/2 cup shredded Swiss cheese
8 slices bacon, crisp-cooked and crumbled
1/2 cup toasted walnuts
Dressing (below)

Combine the spinach, cheese, bacon and walnuts in a salad bowl. Toss to mix. Add the Dressing and toss to coat. **Serves 4 to 6.**

Dressing

1/2 cup sugar
1/2 cup white vinegar
2 tablespoons vegetable oil
1 green onion, finely chopped
1 tablespoon chopped fresh parsley
1 teaspoon mustard
1 teaspoon Worcestershire sauce
1/4 teaspoon pepper

Whisk the sugar, vinegar, oil, green onion, parsley, mustard, Worcestershire sauce and pepper in a bowl.

Blueberry Gelatin Salad

1 (6-ounce) package cherry gelatin

2 cups boiling water

1 (21-ounce) can blueberry pie filling

1 (15-ounce) can crushed pineapple, drained

8 ounces cream cheese, softened

$^{1}/_{2}$ cup sugar

1 cup sour cream

1 teaspoon vanilla extract

Dissolve the gelatin in the boiling water in a large bowl. Stir in the pie filling and pineapple. Pour into a 9×13-inch baking dish. Chill until set. Beat the cream cheese, sugar, sour cream and vanilla in a bowl. Spread over the gelatin. **Serves 8 to 10.**

Cranberry Salad

1 (12-ounce) bag fresh cranberries, finely chopped

1 cup sugar

2 pounds seedless red grapes

1 cup chopped pecans

1 to $1^{1}/_{2}$ cups miniature marshmallows

3 cups heavy whipping cream, whipped

Mix the cranberries and sugar in a large bowl. Cover and chill overnight. Stir in the grapes, pecans and marshmallows. Fold in the whipped cream. Cover and chill for 1 to 2 hours. **Serves 8.**

Grape Salad

  1 bunch seedless green grapes, stemmed, rinsed and dried
  1 bunch seedless red grapes, stemmed, rinsed and dried
  1 cup pecan halves
  1^{1}/$_{2}$ cups sour cream
  1 cup packed brown sugar
  1 teaspoon almond extract

Place the green grapes and red grapes in a large bowl. Sprinkle with the pecans. Mix the sour cream, brown sugar and almond extract in a bowl. Add to the grapes and stir gently to mix. Cover and chill overnight. Serve in compote glasses. **Serves 6 to 8.**

Grilled Pear Salad

1 cup walnut halves

2 cups ruby port

1 shallot, sliced

1 cup olive oil

3 tablespoons red wine vinegar

Salt and pepper to taste

3 Bosc pears, cored and cut into $1/4$-inch slices

12 cups mixed baby greens

8 ounces bacon, crisp-cooked and crumbled

$3/4$ cup crumbled Roquefort cheese

Spread the walnuts on a baking sheet. Bake at 350 degrees for 5 minutes or until toasted. Remove to a wire rack to cool. Bring the port and shallot to a boil in a heavy saucepan. Reduce the heat to medium-low. Simmer for 10 minutes or until the liquid is reduced to $1/2$ cup. Pour through a wire-mesh strainer into a large bowl and let cool. Whisk in the olive oil and vinegar. Season with salt and pepper. Spray the pear slices lightly with nonstick cooking spray. Grill or broil for 2 minutes per side or until light brown in spots. Add the greens, bacon, cheese, walnuts and pears to the port mixture. Toss gently to coat. **Serves 6.**

Spring Pear Salad

2 cup shredded lettuce
2^1/$_2$ cups grated carrots
5 pear halves, cored
10 (^{1}/$_2$-inch) balls cream cheese
Finely chopped fresh parsley
10 (^{1}/$_2$-inch) balls American cheese
^{1}/$_3$ cup French salad dressing

Arrange the lettuce on 5 salad plates. Make a nest of carrots on top of the lettuce. Place 1 pear half on each carrot nest. Roll the cream cheese balls in chopped parsley. Place 2 cream cheese balls and 2 American cheese balls in each pear half. Drizzle the salad dressing over the top. **Serves 5.**

Café Salad

1 head green leaf lettuce or red leaf lettuce
1 head Boston lettuce or butter lettuce
1 red bell pepper, cut into thin strips
1 (16-ounce) package sliced fresh mushrooms
1 (4 to 6-ounce) package crumbled blue cheese
1 heaping cup toasted walnuts
Cherry tomatoes, halved
Dressing (below)

Combine the leaf lettuce, Boston lettuce, bell pepper, mushrooms, cheese, walnuts and cherry tomatoes in a large salad bowl. Toss to mix. Add the Dressing and toss to coat. **Serves 8.**

Dressing

$3/4$ cup olive oil
$1/4$ cup balsamic vinegar
2 to 3 garlic cloves, minced
1 shallot, chopped
1 tablespoon spicy Dijon mustard
Salt to taste
Seasoned pepper to taste
Freshly ground black pepper to taste

Whisk the olive oil, vinegar, garlic, shallot and mustard in a bowl. Season with salt, seasoned pepper and black pepper to taste. Cover and chill for at least 24 hours.

Tangy Red Wine Vinegar Salad Dressing

1/4 cup plus 2 tablespoons mayonnaise

2 tablespoons red wine vinegar

1 tablespoon olive oil

1/4 teaspoon garlic powder

1/4 teaspoon freshly ground pepper

1/8 teaspoon crushed oregano

1 (4-ounce) jar sliced pimentos, drained

Whisk the mayonnaise, vinegar, olive oil, garlic powder, pepper and oregano in a bowl. Cover and chill thoroughly. Stir in the pimentos just before serving. Use on pasta salad, spinach salad, chicken salad or house salads. **Makes 3/4 cup.**

Honey Lime Salad Dressing

1/4 cup Dijon mustard

1/4 teaspoon ginger

1 cup mayonnaise

1/4 cup honey

1/4 cup lime juice

3 tablespoons sesame oil

Mix the mustard and ginger in a bowl. Stir in the mayonnaise, honey, lime juice and sesame oil. Cover and chill. Serve over salad greens or fruit. **Makes 1 3/4 cups.**

"After a good dinner one can forgive
anybody, even one's own relatives."

—Oscar Wilde

Elegant Entrées

Wasabi Brisket

3 tablespoons brown sugar
2 tablespoons Chinese 5-spice powder
2 tablespoons cumin
2 tablespoons sweet paprika
2 garlic cloves, pressed
2^1/2 teaspoons salt
1 (3-inch) piece fresh ginger, finely
   chopped
1 tablespoon wasabi powder
1 tablespoon pepper

1 teaspoon coriander
1 (4-pound) beef brisket, trimmed
^{1}/2 cup soy sauce
3 tablespoons Thai garlic chile
   pepper sauce
3 tablespoons wasabi paste
3 tablespoons brown sugar
2 garlic cloves, pressed
1 tablespoon Dijon mustard
Salt and pepper to taste

Mix 3 tablespoons brown sugar, the 5-spice powder, cumin, paprika, 2 garlic cloves, 2^1/2 teaspoons salt, ginger, wasabi powder, pepper and coriander in a small bowl. Rub the spice mixture into all sides of the brisket. Line a 9×13-inch baking pan with foil, leaving a 7-inch overhang on each side. Place the brisket, fat side up, in the pan. Seal the foil. Chill for at least 8 hours. Let stand at room temperature for 30 minutes. Bake at 350 degrees for 1 hour. Reduce the heat to 275 degrees. Bake for 4 to 4^1/2 hours or until the meat is just tender. Remove from the oven and let stand for 20 minutes. Open the foil and remove the brisket to a cutting board. Slice the meat thinly against the grain, cutting almost through but leaving the bottom attached. Place back in the foil. Whisk the soy sauce, garlic, chile pepper sauce, wasabi paste, 3 tablespoons brown sugar, 2 garlic cloves and the mustard in a bowl. Season with salt and pepper. Pour over the brisket and reseal the foil. Bake at 275 degrees for 45 minutes to 1 hour or until fork-tender. **Serves 12.**

Slow-Cooker Beer Brisket

1 (18-ounce) bottle barbecue sauce
1¹/₂ cups apple cider vinegar
2 cups water
1 (12-ounce) can beer
1 cup light corn syrup
3 tablespoons mustard
Tabasco sauce to taste
Worcestershire sauce to taste
Garlic powder to taste
Salt and pepper to taste
1 (3- to 4-pound) beef brisket, trimmed

Mix the barbecue sauce, vinegar, water, beer, corn syrup and mustard in a saucepan. Season with Tabasco sauce, Worcestershire sauce, garlic powder, salt and pepper. Cook over medium heat until hot, stirring often. Place the brisket, fat side up, in a roasting pan. Pour the marinade over the meat. Cover and chill for at least 24 hours, turning at least 2 or 3 times during marinating. Remove the meat and marinade to a large slow cooker. Cook on Low for 8 to 10 hours or until tender. **Serves 6 to 8.**

Marinated Flank Steak

 2 pounds flank steak
 4 cups Dr Pepper soda
 1/2 cup vegetable oil
 Seasoning Blend (below)

Place the steak in a shallow baking dish. Pour the Dr Pepper over the steak. Cover and marinate in the refrigerator for at least 6 hours. Remove the meat and discard the marinade. Coat the meat with the oil. Sprinkle both sides of the meat with Seasoning Blend. Grill for 3 minutes per side for medium-rare. Remove to a cutting board and slice against the grain. Serve with tortillas, if desired. **Serves 6 to 8.**

Seasoning Blend

 1/4 cup kosher salt
 3 tablespoons ancho pasilla powder or chili powder
 2 tablespoons granulated garlic
 2 tablespoons sugar
 2 tablespoons cumin
 2 tablespoons coarsely ground pepper
 1 tablespoon ground thyme

Combine the salt, ancho pasilla powder, garlic, sugar, cumin, pepper and thyme in a small bowl. Stir to mix well. Store in an airtight container.

Peppered Beef Tenderloin with Mustard and Horseradish Sauce

2 tablespoons whole black peppercorns

2 teaspoons coarse salt

3 tablespoons Dijon mustard

2 tablespoons butter, softened

1 cup loosely packed fresh Italian parsley, chopped;
    or 1/2 cup parsley, chopped, and 1/2 cup rosemary, chopped

1 (2-pound) beef tenderloin, eye roast or round roast, trimmed

Fresh parsley sprigs

Mustard and Horseradish Sauce (below)

Grind the peppercorns coarsely onto waxed paper. Add the salt and stir to mix. Whisk the mustard, butter and parsley in a bowl. Rub the mustard mixture into all sides of the tenderloin. Roll in the pepper mixture to coat. Cover and chill for up to 24 hours, if desired. Place the tenderloin on a rack in a shallow roasting pan. Roast at 450 degrees for 35 minutes or to 130 degrees on a meat thermometer inserted in the center for rare. Remove the meat to a cutting board and cover. Let stand for 10 minutes. Slice the meat and arrange on a platter. Surround with parsley sprigs. Serve with the Mustard and Horseradish Sauce. **Serves 4.**

Mustard and Horseradish Sauce

1 cup sour cream

3 tablespoons Dijon mustard

2 tablespoons prepared horseradish

Whisk the sour cream, mustard and horseradish in a small bowl. Cover and chill for up to 2 days.

Grilled Chuck Roast

1 (4- to 5-pound) chuck roast
Meat tenderizer
4 (or more) garlic cloves, crushed
1 tablespoon brown sugar
1/4 cup soy sauce

2 tablespoons water
1/2 teaspoon ginger
1 tablespoon Worcestershire sauce
1 tablespoon sherry or wine
1 tablespoon vegetable oil

Sprinkle the roast liberally with meat tenderizer. Pierce both sides of the meat with a fork and place in a shallow baking dish. Mix the garlic, brown sugar, soy sauce, water, ginger, Worcestershire sauce, sherry and oil in a small bowl. Pour over the meat. Cover and marinate in the refrigerator for several hours, turning frequently. Remove the meat and discard the marinade. Grill over a charcoal fire for 15 minutes per side. Remove to a cutting board and slice diagonally against the grain. **Serves 8.**

Note: Slice the meat thinly for sandwiches.

The 500-Degree Roast

1 standing rib roast, prime rib roast or
    beef tenderloin
Minced garlic to taste
Chopped fresh rosemary to taste

Salt and pepper to taste
Shiitake Mushroom Cream Sauce or
    Bordelaise Sauce (page 111)

Let the roast come to room temperature. Season with garlic, rosemary, salt and pepper and place in a shallow roasting pan. Roast at 500 degrees for 5 minutes per pound. Turn off the oven and leave the roast in the oven for 2 hours for medium-rare; do not open the oven door. Serve with Shiitake Mushroom Cream Sauce or Bordelaise Sauce. Allow 8 ounces of uncooked beef per person.

Shiitake Mushroom Cream Sauce

1½ tablespoons grapeseed oil

2 garlic cloves, minced

¼ cup chopped onion

10 to 12 shiitake mushrooms, chopped

1 cup heavy cream or half-and-half

1 tablespoon soy sauce

Salt and pepper to taste

Chopped fresh thyme or rosemary
to taste

Chicken broth (optional)

Heat the oil in a saucepan. Add the garlic and onion and sauté until tender. Add the mushrooms and sauté until the mushrooms are tender. Stir in the cream and soy sauce. Season with salt and pepper. Cook until the cream is reduced and slightly thickened. Season with thyme and cook for 1 minute, stirring often. Add chicken broth if necessary to thin the sauce. Serve over pasta, chicken, beef tenderloin or prime rib. **Serves 4.**

Bordelaise Sauce

¼ cup (½ stick) butter

2 shallots, chopped

2 garlic cloves, minced

2 thin onion slices

2 carrots, sliced

2 fresh parsley sprigs

10 whole peppercorns

2 cloves

2 bay leaves

3 tablespoons all-purpose flour

1 (10½-ounce) can beef broth

¾ cup red bordeaux

¼ teaspoon salt

¼ teaspoon pepper

2 tablespoons finely chopped
fresh parsley

¼ cup red bordeaux

Melt the butter in a saucepan. Add the shallots, garlic, onion, carrots, parsley sprigs, peppercorns, cloves and bay leaves. Sauté until the vegetables are tender. Remove from the heat and stir in the flour. Cook over low heat until the flour is light brown, stirring constantly. Remove from the heat and stir in the broth and ¾ cup bordeaux. Bring to a boil, stirring constantly. Pour the sauce through a wire-mesh strainer into a bowl. Discard the solids. Stir in the salt, pepper, chopped parsley and ¼ cup bordeaux.
Serves 4.

McLendon Chisholm Grand Champion Chili

5 to 6 pounds ground chuck

2 onions, chopped

1 celery rib, chopped

2 (10-ounce) cans diced tomatoes with green chiles

1 (23-ounce) can ranch-style beans

1 (46-ounce) can tomato juice

3/4 cup lemon juice

6 tablespoons vinegar

1 1/3 cups ketchup

1 tablespoon salt

2 teaspoons dry mustard

1/2 cup packed brown sugar

2 1/2 tablespoons chili powder

2 1/2 tablespoons Worcestershire sauce

1 jalapeño chile, sliced

Brown the ground chuck in a large saucepan, stirring until crumbly; drain. Stir in the onions, celery, tomatoes with green chiles, beans, tomato juice, lemon juice, vinegar, ketchup, salt, dry mustard, brown sugar, chili powder, Worcestershire sauce and jalapeño. Bring to a boil and reduce the heat. Simmer for 30 minutes, stirring often. Serve with crackers or corn bread. **Serves 12.**

Note: For the best flavor, make a day ahead and chill. Reheat when ready to serve.

Mexican Casserole

$1^{1}/2$ pounds ground beef

1 small onion, chopped

1 (15-ounce) can mild or hot enchilada sauce

1 (4-ounce) can chopped green chiles

1 ($10^{3}/4$-ounce) can condensed cream of mushroom or cream of chicken soup

1 ($10^{3}/4$-ounce) can condensed cream of onion soup

$^{2}/3$ cup milk

1 bag Doritos, crumbled

1 pound Velveeta cheese, shredded

Brown the ground beef in a large saucepan with the onion, stirring until the ground beef is crumbly; drain. Stir in the enchilada sauce and green chiles. Mix the mushroom soup, onion soup and milk in a saucepan. Cook until hot, stirring occasionally. Spread $^{1}/3$ of the tortilla chips in a 3-quart casserole dish. Sprinkle with $^{1}/2$ of the cheese and top with $^{1}/2$ of the meat mixture. Pour $^{1}/2$ the soup mixture over the meat layer. Repeat the layers and top with the remaining Doritos. Bake at 350 degrees for 30 to 35 minutes or until bubbly. **Serves 8 to 10.**

Taco Rocks

1 pound ground beef
1 small onion, chopped
1 envelope taco seasoning mix
$^3/4$ cup water
$^1/2$ cup ketchup
1 (2$^1/4$-ounce) can sliced black olives
1 (8-ounce) can refrigerator crescent rolls
1 cup shredded Monterey Jack cheese
Shredded lettuce
Diced tomatoes
Diced avocado
Shredded Cheddar cheese
Sour cream

Brown the ground beef in a large saucepan with the onion, stirring until the ground beef is crumbly; drain. Stir in the taco seasoning mix, water, ketchup and olives. Simmer for 10 to 15 minutes. Unroll the crescent dough on a lightly floured work surface. Separate into 4 rectangles and roll out with a rolling pin to seal the seams. Mound $^1/4$ of the meat mixture in the center of each rectangle. Top each with $^1/4$ of the Monterey Jack cheese. Join the corners of the dough together to seal each packet. Place on a nonstick baking sheet. Bake according to the crescent roll package directions. Arrange a bed of lettuce on each of 4 serving plates. Sprinkle with tomatoes and avocado. Top with a Taco Rock. Sprinkle with Cheddar cheese and top with a dollop of sour cream. **Serves 4.**

Terrific Taco Pie

1 pound lean ground beef

$1/2$ onion, chopped

1 (8-ounce) can tomato sauce

1 ($1^1/2$-ounce) envelope taco seasoning mix

$1/3$ cup chopped black olives

1 (8-ounce) can refrigerator crescent rolls

2 cups crushed corn chips

1 cup sour cream, at room temperature

1 cup shredded Cheddar cheese

Shredded lettuce

Chopped tomato

Sliced avocado

Picante sauce

Brown the ground beef in a large skillet over medium heat with the onion, stirring until the ground beef is crumbly; drain. Stir in the tomato sauce, taco seasoning mix and olives. Simmer for 15 minutes. Separate the crescent dough into 8 triangles and arrange in a 9-inch pie plate, pressing the seams together to form a pie shell. Sprinkle $1/2$ of the corn chips over the dough. Spread the meat mixture evenly over the corn chips and spread the sour cream over the meat mixture. (May be frozen at this point for later use. Thaw before continuing.) Top with the cheese and sprinkle with the remaining corn chips. Bake at 375 degrees for 20 to 25 minutes. Cut into wedges and place on serving plates. Top with lettuce, tomato, avocado and picante sauce. **Serves 6.**

Poor Man's Stroganoff

2 tablespoons butter

$^1/_2$ cup chopped onion

1 garlic clove, minced

2 pounds ground beef

2 tablespoons all-purpose flour

2 teaspoons salt

$^1/_4$ teaspoon pepper

$^1/_2$ teaspoon tarragon

$^1/_4$ teaspoon basil

1 (6-ounce) can tomato paste

1 (10$^1/_2$-ounce) can beef consommé

1 tablespoon wine vinegar

1 cup sour cream

1 (8-ounce) package fresh mushrooms, cleaned and sliced

6 ounces egg noodles, cooked al dente and drained

Melt the butter in a large saucepan. Add the onion and garlic and sauté for 5 minutes. Add the ground beef and cook until light brown, stirring until crumbly; drain. Sprinkle the flour, salt, pepper, tarragon and basil over the meat mixture. Stir in the tomato paste, consommé and vinegar. Simmer for 10 minutes. Remove from the heat and stir in the sour cream, mushrooms and noodles. **Serves 6 to 8.**

Hungarian Stuffed Peppers

3 tablespoons vegetable oil

1 large onion, finely chopped

8 ounces ground beef

8 ounces ground pork

1 cup rice

2 teaspoons salt

$^1/_2$ teaspoon pepper

8 green bell peppers

1 (14-ounce) can tomato juice

1 cup sour cream

Heat the oil in a skillet. Add the onion and sauté until tender. Remove to a large bowl.
Add the ground beef, ground pork, rice, salt and pepper. Stir to mix well. Cut the tops
off the bell peppers and remove the seeds. Fill the bell peppers with the meat mixture
to $^1/_4$ inch from the top. Place the stuffed peppers in a roasting pan, arranging so the
peppers remain upright. Pour the tomato juice over the stuffed peppers. Bake at
350 degrees for 1 hour or until the rice is tender and the meat is cooked through.
Add the sour cream and shake the pan gently to mix. **Serves 8.**

German Cabbage Rolls

1 large head cabbage, cored
1¹/₂ pounds ground beef
1 onion, chopped
4 ounces uncooked rice
Salt and pepper to taste
2 (14-ounce) cans sauerkraut
2 cups tomato juice
2 cups sour cream

Pour boiling water over the head of cabbage in a bowl. Let stand until the leaves soften. Separate the leaves and place on a work surface. Mix the ground beef, onion and rice in a bowl. Season with salt and pepper. Shape into 1¹/₂-inch balls. Wrap each ball in a cabbage leaf and secure with a wooden pick. Spread a layer of sauerkraut in the bottom of a large heavy saucepan. Add a layer of cabbage rolls. Continue layering sauerkraut and cabbage rolls, ending with cabbage rolls. Pour the tomato juice over the top and add water to cover, if needed. Arrange a layer of cabbage leaves on top. Simmer for 2 hours or until the rice is tender and the meat is cooked through. Serve with the sour cream. **Serves 8.**

English Shepherd's Pie

2 pounds ground beef

$^1/_2$ onion, chopped

Salt and pepper to taste

1 (10$^3/_4$-ounce) can condensed cream of mushroom soup

1 (12-ounce) jar beef gravy

2 (10-ounce) packages frozen green peas, cooked and drained

12 servings prepared instant mashed potatoes

2 cups shredded Cheddar cheese (optional)

6 slices bacon, crisp-cooked and crumbled (optional)

2 tablespoons chopped fresh parsley (optional)

Brown the ground beef in a large skillet over medium heat with the onion, stirring until the ground beef is crumbly; drain. Season with salt and pepper. Remove to a 9×13-inch baking dish. Add the soup and stir to mix well. Spread the mixture in the baking dish. Pour the gravy evenly over the top. Sprinkle with the peas. Spread the mashed potatoes over the peas. Sprinkle with the cheese, bacon and parsley. Bake at 350 degrees for 45 to 50 minutes or until golden brown. **Serves 10 to 12.**

Bobotie

2 onions, thinly sliced
2 tablespoons vegetable oil
1 tablespoon curry powder
1 teaspoon turmeric
2 tablespoons white vinegar or lemon
    juice
1 tablespoon sugar
1 teaspoon salt
1/2 teaspoon pepper
1 slice white bread
1 cup milk

2 pounds ground beef, or 1 pound
    ground beef and 1 pound
    ground lamb
1 egg
1/2 cup raisins
3 tablespoons chutney
Grated zest of 1 lemon (optional)
2 bay leaves
6 to 12 blanched almonds, quartered
Milk
1 egg

Boil the onions in a small amount of water in a saucepan just until opaque. Drain the onions, reserving the water. Chop the onions. Heat the oil in a skillet. Add the onions and cook until golden brown, stirring constantly. Add the curry powder and turmeric and cook for 2 minutes, stirring constantly. Stir in the vinegar, sugar, salt and pepper. Remove from the heat. Soak the bread in 1 cup milk in a small bowl. Remove the bread and squeeze dry. Set aside. Strain the milk though a wire-mesh strainer and set aside. Crumble the ground beef into a skillet. Add the reserved onion water and a small amount of boiling water. Cook for 5 minutes; drain. Combine the cooked beef, soaked bread, onion mixture, 1 egg, raisins, chutney and lemon zest in a large bowl. Stir gently to mix. Pack into a buttered baking dish and top with the bay leaves. Bake, covered, at 350 degrees for 1 1/2 hours. Insert the almonds into the meat mixture. Add enough milk to the reserved strained milk to make 1 cup. Whisk the milk and 1 egg in a bowl. Pour over the meat mixture carefully to make a smooth layer. Bake, uncovered, at 325 degrees for 30 minutes or until the custard layer is set. **Serves 8.**

Lamb Chops with Raisin Spice Sauce

^{1}/2 cup (1 stick) unsalted butter

24 lamb chops

Garlic powder to taste

Salt to taste

Tarragon to taste

4 shallots, chopped

1 cup heavy cream

^{1}/2 to 1 teaspoon good-quality curry powder

4 handfuls raisins

^{1}/2 to 1 teaspoon tarragon

Melt 2 tablespoons of the butter in a large skillet over medium-high heat. Add 6 of the lamb chops and brown on both sides. Reduce the heat to medium-low. Season the lamb with garlic powder, salt and tarragon. Cook the lamb until barely pink inside. Remove to a platter and cover with foil. Repeat with the remaining lamb, using 2 tablespoons butter and 6 lamb chops for each batch. Place in a 200-degree oven. Add the shallots to the pan drippings and sauté until tender. Stir in the cream. Add the curry powder, raisins and ^{1}/2 to 1 teaspoon tarragon. Season with additional garlic powder and salt. Cook until thickened, stirring often. Add the juices from the platter of lamb chops. Place the lamb chops on serving plates and cover with the sauce. **Serves 8.**

Luscious Lamb

8 lamb chops
Garlic powder to taste
2 tablespoons butter
2 tablespoons Worcestershire sauce
2 tablespoons lemon juice
2 tablespoons gin
1 teaspoon seasoned salt

Rub the lamb chops with a small amount of garlic powder and place in a shallow baking dish. Melt the butter in a small saucepan. Stir in the Worcestershire sauce, lemon juice, gin and seasoned salt. Pour over the lamb. Cover and marinate in the refrigerator for 30 minutes. Remove the lamb and pour the marinade into a small saucepan. Boil the marinade for 10 minutes. Broil or grill the lamb chops to desired doneness. Serve the lamb topped with the marinade. **Serves 4.**

Stuffed Pork Chops with Sweet Sour Sauce

1½ cups seasoned stuffing mix
1 cup applesauce
½ teaspoon nutmeg
½ cup boiling water
6 (1¼-inch-thick) pork chops
Salt and pepper to taste
Sweet Sour Sauce (below)

Stir the stuffing mix, applesauce and nutmeg in a bowl. Add the water and stir to mix well. Make a slit to the bone in the side of each pork chop. Season with salt and pepper. Fill the cavities with the stuffing mixture. Brown the pork in a nonstick skillet for 5 to 10 minutes per side. Remove to a baking dish. Bake at 375 degrees for 1 hour, turning the pork chops every 15 minutes and basting with the sauce. **Serves 6.**

Sweet Sour Sauce

1 cup sugar
2 tablespoons cornstarch
½ teaspoon salt
¼ teaspoon ginger
1 (6-ounce) can pineapple juice
½ cup white wine vinegar
½ cup lemon juice

Mix the sugar, cornstarch, salt and ginger in a saucepan. Stir in the pineapple juice, vinegar and lemon juice. Cook until thick and clear, stirring often.

Grilled Pork Chops with Pineapple Salsa

4 (³/4-inch-thick, 4-ounce) boneless center-cut loin pork chops
Vegetable oil
Salt and pepper to taste
Pineapple Salsa (below)

Brush the pork chops lightly with oil on both sides. Season with salt and pepper. Grill, covered, over high heat for 6 minutes on the first side and 5 minutes, uncovered, or with lid open on the other side or until cooked through; do not overcook. Remove to serving plates and top with some of the Pineapple Salsa. Serve any remaining salsa on the side. **Serves 4.**

Pineapple Salsa

1 very ripe tomato
1 (8-ounce) can pineapple tidbits packed in juice, drained
2 tablespoons grated onion
2 to 3 sprigs of cilantro or parsley, chopped
1 tablespoon bottled unsweetened lime juice
¹/8 teaspoon salt
¹/8 teaspoon crushed red pepper

Core and chop the tomato into bite-size pieces on a cutting board. Remove the tomato and juice to a 2-quart bowl. Stir in the pineapple, onion, cilantro, lime juice, salt and crushed red pepper. Serve immediately.

Herb-Rubbed Pork Tenderloin

2 teaspoons rosemary, crushed
2 teaspoons thyme, crushed
2 teaspoons cumin
1 teaspoon coarsely ground pepper
1 teaspoon garlic salt
1 (2- to 2$^{1}/_{2}$-pound) pork tenderloin

Mix the rosemary, thyme, cumin, pepper and garlic salt in a small bowl. Rub into all sides of the pork tenderloin. Place the pork in a baking pan coated with nonstick cooking spray. Bake at 375 degrees for 40 to 45 minutes or until cooked through. Let stand for 5 minutes before slicing. **Serves 6.**

Grilled Pork Tenderloin

2 to 2¹/₂ pounds pork tenderloins
¹/₄ cup bourbon
¹/₄ cup soy sauce
¹/₄ cup vegetable oil
¹/₄ cup packed brown sugar
¹/₄ cup Dijon mustard
3 garlic cloves, minced
1 teaspoon Worcestershire sauce
¹/₄ teaspoon ginger

Place the pork tenderloins in a shallow baking dish. Mix the bourbon, soy sauce, oil, brown sugar, mustard, garlic, Worcestershire sauce and ginger in a bowl. Pour over the pork. Cover and marinate in the refrigerator for at least 1 hour. Remove the pork and discard the marinade. Grill the pork tenderloins 4 inches above medium-hot coals for 15 to 25 minutes or until cooked through. **Serves 4 to 6.**

Tequila-Marinated Pork Tenderloin

2 (1-pound) pork tenderloins
4 garlic cloves, sliced
3 tablespoons fresh rosemary, chopped
1½ cups vegetable oil
1 cup tequila
¼ cup fresh lime juice
1 tablespoon pepper
2 teaspoons salt

Make small slits in the pork tenderloins and insert the garlic slices. Place the pork in a shallow baking dish. Sprinkle with the rosemary. Mix the oil, tequila, lime juice, pepper and salt in a bowl. Pour over the pork. Cover and marinate in the refrigerator for 8 to 10 hours. Remove the pork and discard the marinade. Grill the pork for 15 to 20 minutes or until cooked through, turning occasionally to cook evenly. **Serves 4.**

Grilled Pork Loin with Peaches on Fettuccini

$1/4$ cup ($1/2$ stick) unsalted butter

3 tablespoons brown sugar

1 tablespoon honey

$1/2$ cup chicken stock

1 pinch of nutmeg

1 pinch of cinnamon

2 cups sliced peeled fresh peaches or frozen peaches, thawed

1 (3- to 4-pound) pork loin roast

1 tablespoon unsalted butter

1 tablespoon freshly ground pepper

8 ounces fresh fettuccini, cooked al dente and drained

2 tablespoons peach brandy

Melt $1/4$ cup butter in a saucepan. Stir in the brown sugar, honey, chicken stock, nutmeg and cinnamon. Simmer for 3 minutes. Add the peaches and simmer for 10 minutes or until the peaches are soft but not mushy. Grill the pork loin slowly until cooked through, basting occasionally with the peach sauce. Cut the pork into $1/4$-inch slices and place on a platter. Cover with foil and keep warm. Simmer the remaining peach sauce for 5 minutes and remove from the heat. Melt 1 tablespoon butter in a small saucepan. Stir in the pepper. Pour over the fettuccini in a bowl. Toss to coat. Add the brandy to the peach sauce and carefully ignite the brandy. Let the flames burn off. Arrange the fettuccini on serving plates and top with the sliced pork. Pour the peach sauce over the pork. **Serves 6 to 8.**

Apricot-Pecan-Stuffed Pork Loin

1 (5-pound) boneless pork loin roast	Apricot-Pecan Filling (below)
4 teaspoons salt	1 cup bourbon
1/2 teaspoon pepper	1 cup chicken broth
1 teaspoon thyme or sage	3 tablespoons molasses
1/2 teaspoon ground bay leaf	1/4 cup heavy cream
2 garlic cloves	1/4 teaspoon salt

Trim any excess fat from the pork loin. Grind 4 teaspoons salt, the pepper, thyme, bay leaf and garlic in a small food processor. Rub some of the mixture into all sides of the pork, reserving the leftover rub. Cover the meat and chill for 4 hours or overnight. Butterfly the pork on a work surface and flatten with a meat mallet to 1/2-inch thickness. Spread the Apricot-Pecan Filling evenly over the meat. Roll up the pork from the long side. Rub the outside of the pork with the remaining spice rub. Tie the pork with kitchen twine to secure and place in a roasting pan. Bring the bourbon, chicken broth and molasses to a boil in a saucepan. Remove from the heat and carefully ignite the bourbon. Let the flames burn off. Pour over the pork. Bake at 350 degrees for 1 to 1 1/2 hours or to 160 degrees on a meat thermometer inserted in the pork. Remove the pork to a platter. Cover and keep warm. Add the cream and 1/4 teaspoon salt to the pan drippings. Cook over medium-high heat until slightly thickened, stirring constantly. Slice the pork and serve with the sauce. **Serves 12 to 14.**

Apricot-Pecan Filling

1 1/2 cups dried apricots	1/4 teaspoon pepper
1/2 cup pecans	1 tablespoon thyme
1 garlic clove	1/4 cup molasses
1/2 teaspoon salt	1/4 cup canola or peanut oil

Combine the apricots, pecans, garlic, salt and pepper in a food processor. Process until coarsely chopped. Add 1/2 of the thyme, 1/2 of the molasses and 1/2 of the oil. Process just until mixed. Add the remaining thyme, molasses and oil and process until finely chopped but not smooth.

Pork Barbecue Sandwiches

1 (3-pound) bone-in pork loin roast

Salt and pepper to taste

1 cup chopped onion

1 cup chopped celery

1 (18-ounce) bottle ketchup

2 tablespoons Worcestershire sauce

3 tablespoons cider vinegar

1 tablespoon prepared mustard

Sugar to taste

Sandwich buns or rolls

Season the pork with salt and pepper. Brown the pork on all sides in a large heavy nonstick saucepan. Stir in the onion, celery, ketchup, Worcestershire sauce, vinegar and mustard. Season with sugar. Simmer, covered, for 4 to 5 hours. Remove the pork to a work surface. Remove the meat from the bones and discard the bones and any visible fat. Shred the meat with a fork and return the meat to the saucepan. Stir to mix. Serve on buns at casual buffets and football parties. **Serves 12.**

Note: This can be made ahead and refrigerated or frozen.

Muffuletta Sandwich

3 cups chopped fresh mushrooms
  (about 8 ounces)

1 (8-ounce) can pimento-stuffed
  green olives, drained and chopped

1 (8-ounce) can black olives,
  drained and chopped

1 (4-ounce) jar marinated artichoke
  hearts, drained and chopped

1 (3-ounce) jar cocktail onions,
  drained and chopped

1/2 cup chopped celery

1/4 cup chopped green bell pepper

2/3 cup white vinegar

2/3 cup olive oil

2 1/2 teaspoons Italian seasoning

1 teaspoon garlic powder

1 teaspoon onion powder

1/2 teaspoon pepper

2 (16-ounce) loaves unsliced Italian or
  French bread

8 ounces thinly sliced ham

8 ounces thinly sliced Genoa salami

4 ounces sliced Swiss cheese

4 ounces sliced provolone cheese

Mix the mushrooms, green olives, black olives, artichokes, onions, celery and bell pepper in a large bowl. Combine the vinegar, olive oil, Italian seasoning, garlic powder, onion powder and pepper in a small saucepan. Bring to a boil and boil for 2 to 3 minutes. Pour over the vegetables and stir to mix well. Slice the bread loaves in half lengthwise. Hollow out the bottom halves slightly, if desired. Spread the vegetable mixture on the bottom half of each loaf. Layer the ham, salami, Swiss cheese and provolone cheese on top of the vegetables. Cover with the top half of the loaf. Wrap each loaf in foil and place on a baking sheet. Bake at 375 degrees for 20 minutes or until heated through. Cut the loaves into slices. **Serves 12.**

Oven-Fried Chicken

2 egg whites
1 cup buttermilk
2 teaspoons Tabasco sauce
1 cup all-purpose flour
2 tablespoons baking powder
4 teaspoons paprika
2 teaspoons thyme
2 teaspoons oregano
2 teaspoons salt
$1/2$ teaspoon pepper
5 pounds chicken pieces, skin and fat removed

Whisk the egg whites, buttermilk and Tabasco sauce in a medium bowl. Combine the flour, baking powder, paprika, thyme, oregano, salt and pepper in a large sealable plastic bag. Seal the bag and shake to mix. Dip the chicken pieces, 1 at a time, in the buttermilk mixture and then place in the bag. Seal the bag and shake to coat. Arrange the chicken pieces on a broiler pan coated with nonstick cooking spray. Spray nonstick cooking spray over the chicken pieces. Bake at 425 degrees for 35 to 40 minutes or until golden brown and cooked through. **Serves 6.**

Note: This chicken has all the flavor of fried chicken without the fat.

Honolulu Chicken

All-purpose flour for dredging
1/4 teaspoon salt
1/4 teaspoon pepper
1 chicken, cut up
Vegetable oil for frying
1 (10-ounce) jar peach preserves
1/2 cup barbecue sauce
1/2 cup chopped onion
2 tablespoons soy sauce
1 green bell pepper, cut into small strips
1 (6-ounce) can sliced water chestnuts
Hot cooked rice

Mix flour and the salt and pepper in a shallow dish. Dredge the chicken in the flour mixture. Heat oil in a large skillet. Add the chicken and brown on all sides. Mix the peach preserves, barbecue sauce, onion and soy sauce in a bowl. Pour over the chicken in the skillet. Simmer, covered, for 40 minutes. Stir in the bell pepper and simmer for 10 minutes or until the chicken is cooked through. Stir in the water chestnuts and cook until heated through. Serve over rice. **Serves 4.**

Bourbon Chicken

6 boneless skinless chicken breasts

1 teaspoon garlic powder

$^1/_2$ teaspoon pepper

$^1/_4$ cup bourbon

$^1/_4$ cup soy sauce

1 (8-ounce) can crushed pineapple packed in juice

Sprinkle the chicken with the garlic powder and pepper. Arrange in a 9×13-inch baking dish. Mix the bourbon and soy sauce in a small bowl. Pour over the chicken. Cover and marinate in the refrigerator for several hours. Spread the undrained pineapple over the chicken. Bake at 350 degrees for 45 minutes or until the chicken is cooked through, basting several times during cooking. **Serves 6.**

City News Chicken

All-purpose flour for dredging
Salt and pepper to taste
6 to 8 boneless chicken breasts
3 tablespoons butter
Fresh or dried dillweed
Fresh Parmesan, Romano or Asadero cheese, grated
8 ounces fresh mushrooms, sliced
$1/2$ to $2/3$ cup sherry

Place flour in a sealable plastic bag. Season with salt and pepper. Add the chicken and seal the bag. Shake to coat the chicken. Melt the butter in a large skillet over medium heat. Add the chicken. Crush dillweed over the chicken. Turn to brown on the other side and crush dillweed over the chicken. Cook for 5 minutes or until golden brown. Reduce the heat to low. Season with salt, pepper and a generous amount of cheese. Stir in the mushrooms and sherry. Cook, covered, for 15 minutes or until the chicken is cooked through. **Serves 6 to 8.**

Northern Italian Chicken Rolls

4 slices dry bread

4 boneless chicken breasts

Olive oil

4 slices prosciutto

4 slices provolone cheese

1 cup all-purpose flour

2 eggs

Olive oil

$^1/4$ cup ($^1/2$ stick) butter

6 shallots, sliced

8 ounces mushrooms, sliced

$^1/2$ cup all-purpose flour

$1^1/2$ cups chicken broth

2 tablespoons dry marsala

2 tablespoons dry white wine

Hot cooked rice or flat noodles

Grind the bread in a food processor fitted with a steel blade to make crumbs. Spread on a baking sheet and dry in a moderate oven. Remove to a shallow dish. Coat the chicken lightly with olive oil and place in a large sealable plastic bag. Pound lightly with a meat mallet to $^1/2$-inch thickness. Place the chicken on a work surface. Top each chicken breast with 1 slice of prosciutto and 1 slice of cheese. Roll up each chicken breast. Place 1 cup flour in a shallow dish. Beat the eggs in a shallow dish. Dredge the chicken rolls in the flour and then dip in the eggs. Coat with the bread crumbs. Heat olive oil in a skillet over medium-high heat. Add the chicken rolls and brown on all sides. Remove to a lightly greased 6×9-inch baking pan. Melt the butter in a skillet. Add the shallots and mushrooms and sauté until the vegetables are tender. Whisk $^1/2$ cup flour and the chicken broth in a bowl. Add to the skillet and cook until thickened, stirring constantly. Stir in the marsala and white wine. Pour over the chicken rolls. Bake at 350 degrees for 30 minutes or until the chicken is cooked through. Serve over rice or flat noodles. **Serves 4.**

Chicken Breasts with Lemon Caper Sauce

4 boneless skinless chicken breasts

2 tablespoons all-purpose flour

$^1/_2$ teaspoon salt

1 egg

2 teaspoons olive oil

1 tablespoon butter

2 lemons, cut in half

3 garlic cloves, crushed

$^1/_2$ cup chicken broth

$^1/_4$ cup dry white wine

$1^1/_2$ teaspoons all-purpose flour

2 tablespoons capers, drained

1 tablespoon butter

1 tablespoon chopped fresh parsley

Place the chicken between sheets of waxed paper. Pound with a meat mallet to $^1/_2$-inch thickness. Mix 2 tablespoons flour and the salt in a shallow dish. Beat the egg in a shallow dish. Coat the chicken in the flour mixture and then dip in the egg. Heat the olive oil in a nonstick 12-inch skillet over medium-high heat until very hot. Add the butter and cook until melted. Add the chicken and cook for 5 minutes. Reduce the heat to medium and turn the chicken. Cook for 8 to 10 minutes or until cooked through. Remove the chicken to a platter and keep warm. Cut $^1/_2$ of 1 lemon into thin slices. Add the lemon slices and garlic to the skillet. Sauté until the garlic is golden brown. Squeeze 2 tablespoons juice from the remaining lemons. Stir the lemon juice, chicken broth, wine and $1^1/_2$ teaspoons flour in a small bowl until smooth. Add to the skillet and bring to a boil, stirring constantly. Boil for 1 minute. Stir in the capers and 1 tablespoon butter. Cook until the butter melts, stirring constantly. Remove the garlic and discard. Remove the lemon slices and arrange over the chicken. Pour the sauce over the chicken and sprinkle with the parsley. **Serves 4.**

Chicken Breasts Lombardy

6 whole chicken breasts, boned, skinned and quartered

1/2 cup all-purpose flour

1 cup (2 sticks) butter or margarine

Salt and pepper to taste

1 1/2 cups sliced mushrooms

3/4 cup marsala or dry white wine

1/2 cup chicken stock

1/2 teaspoon salt

1/8 teaspoon pepper

1/2 cup shredded fontina or mozzarella cheese

1/2 cup grated Parmesan cheese

Place the chicken between sheets of waxed paper. Flatten with a meat mallet or rolling pin to 1/8-inch thickness. Dredge the chicken lightly in the flour. Melt 2 tablespoons of the butter in a large skillet over low heat. Add 4 chicken pieces and cook for 3 to 4 minutes per side or until golden brown. Remove the chicken to a greased 9×13-inch baking dish, overlapping the pieces. Season with salt and pepper. Repeat 5 more times to brown the remaining chicken, using 2 tablespoons butter each time. Set aside the skillet and drippings. Melt the remaining 1/4 cup butter in a skillet. Add the mushrooms and sauté until tender; drain. Sprinkle the mushrooms over the chicken. Stir the marsala and chicken stock into the skillet with the chicken pan drippings. Simmer for 10 minutes, stirring occasionally. Stir in 1/2 teaspoon salt and 1/8 teaspoon pepper. Spoon about 1/3 of the sauce over the chicken and reserve the remaining sauce. Mix the fontina cheese and Parmesan cheese in a small bowl. Sprinkle over the chicken. Bake at 450 degrees for 10 to 12 minutes. Place under a broiler for 1 to 2 minutes or until light brown. Serve with the reserved sauce. **Serves 8.**

Note: Turkey breast may be substituted for the chicken.

Chicken Pomodoro

4 chicken cutlets
Salt and pepper to taste
All-purpose flour for dredging
2 tablespoons vegetable oil
1/4 cup vodka
1/2 cup chicken broth
2 tablespoons fresh lemon juice
1/2 cup chopped tomatoes
2 tablespoons heavy cream
1/3 cup finely chopped scallions

Season the chicken with salt and pepper and dredge in flour. Heat the oil in a skillet. Add the chicken and sauté until cooked through. Remove the chicken to a platter. Drain the oil from the skillet. Set the skillet on a heatproof surface and add the vodka. Deglaze the skillet, scraping up any browned bits. Return the skillet to the heat and cook until the vodka is almost evaporated. Stir in the chicken broth and lemon juice. Add the chicken and cook for 1 minute per side. Remove the chicken to a warm platter. Add the tomatoes and cream to the skillet. Cook until heated through, stirring often. Pour over the chicken and sprinkle with the scallions. **Serves 2.**

Stuffed Chicken Breasts with Pecan Wild Rice Pilaf

8 to 12 ounces ricotta cheese

8 ounces fresh spinach leaves, finely
    chopped

1 small broccoli floret, finely chopped

Few pinches of thyme

Few pinches of tarragon

Salt and pepper to taste

4 boneless chicken breasts

$^1/_4$ cup ($^1/_2$ stick) butter, cut into
    4 pieces

Combine the cheese, spinach, broccoli, thyme and tarragon in a bowl. Season with
salt and pepper. Stir to mix well. Lift up the skin from the chicken on 1 side of each
chicken breast. Stuff the spinach mixture into the pocket. Fold the skin under the
chicken breast. Place in a roasting pan and top each chicken breast with a piece of
butter. Bake at 350 degrees for 1 hour or until golden brown and cooked through.
Serve hot, whole or sliced, with Pecan Wild Rice Pilaf (below). **Serves 4.**

Pecan Wild Rice Pilaf

4 cups chicken broth

1 cup wild rice, rinsed

$2^1/_4$ cups water

$1^3/_4$ cups wheat pilaf

1 cup pecan halves

1 cup dried currants

1 bunch scallions, thinly sliced

$^1/_2$ cup chopped fresh Italian parsley

$^1/_2$ cup chopped fresh mint leaves

Grated zest of 2 oranges

2 tablespoons olive oil

1 tablespoon orange juice

Pepper to taste

Bring the chicken broth to boil in a saucepan. Stir in the wild rice and return to a boil.
Reduce the heat to medium-low. Cook, covered, for 50 minutes or until the liquid is
absorbed and the rice is tender; do not overcook. Remove to a large bowl. Bring the
water to a boil in a saucepan. Stir in the pilaf. Cover and return to a boil. Reduce the
heat to low and simmer for 15 minutes or until the water is absorbed and the pilaf is
tender. Remove from the heat and let stand for 15 minutes. Add to the wild rice. Add
the pecans, currants, scallions, parsley, mint, orange zest, olive oil and orange juice.
Season with pepper. Toss well to mix. Serve at room temperature. **Serves 8.**

Tortilla-Crusted Chicken Stuffed with Pepper Jack Cheese and Spinach

4 boneless skinless chicken breasts

4 slices Pepper Jack cheese

1 (10-ounce) package frozen chopped spinach, cooked, drained and squeezed dry

1 cup crushed tortilla chips (red, if available)

3/4 teaspoon salt

1/2 teaspoon oregano

1/4 teaspoon cumin

1/4 teaspoon pepper

1 egg

1 tablespoon vegetable or corn oil

Cilantro Pesto (below)

Make a slit in each chicken breast and stuff with the cheese and spinach. Mix the tortilla chips, salt, oregano, cumin and pepper in a shallow dish. Beat the egg in a shallow dish. Dip the chicken in the egg and coat in the tortilla chip mixture. Heat the oil in an ovenproof skillet over medium-high heat. Add the chicken and brown for 3 minutes per side. Reduce the heat to medium-low and cook for 15 to 18 minutes or until the chicken is cooked through, turning once. Serve with Cilantro Pesto. **Serves 4.**

Cilantro Pesto

1/4 cup extra-virgin olive oil

1 cup loosely packed fresh cilantro

2 tablespoons roasted pine nuts

2 large garlic cloves

1 jalapeño chile, seeded and sliced

1/3 cup grated Romano or Parmesan cheese

Combine the olive oil, cilantro, pine nuts, garlic, jalapeño and cheese in a food processor. Process until smooth. Store in an airtight container in the refrigerator for up to 3 to 4 weeks or in the freezer for up to 6 months. **Makes 1 cup.**

Tortilla-Crusted Chicken Paillard with Sacaton Relish

4 boneless skinless chicken breasts
1/4 cup all-purpose flour
1 egg white
1 tablespoon water
1 cup crushed tortilla chips
2 teaspoons vegetable oil
Sacaton Relish (below)

Place the chicken between sheets of waxed paper. Pound with a meat mallet to 1/4-inch thickness. Place the flour in a shallow dish. Beat the egg white and water in a shallow dish. Place the tortilla chips in a shallow dish. Dredge the chicken in the flour, then dip in the egg mixture. Coat with the tortilla chips. Heat the oil in a large nonstick skillet over high heat. Add the chicken and brown for 3 minutes per side. Reduce the heat to medium-low. Cook for 5 minutes per side or until the chicken is cooked through. Remove to a platter and top with Sacaton Relish. **Serves 4.**

Sacaton Relish

3 slices bacon, chopped
1 onion, chopped
2 tomatoes, chopped
1 (4 1/2-ounce) can chopped green chiles
1/4 teaspoon salt
1/4 teaspoon pepper

Sauté the bacon in a saucepan over medium-low heat just until crisp. Add the onion and sauté for 7 minutes or until light brown. Stir in the tomatoes and green chiles. Cook for 3 minutes. Sprinkle with the salt and pepper. Stir to mix well.

Marvelous Mindless Moo-Shu

1 tablespoon peanut oil or vegetable oil

3/4 cup chopped scallions or green onions

1 (8-ounce) bag cabbage coleslaw mix

1/2 cup sliced fresh mushrooms

1/4 cup dry sherry

2 teaspoons cornstarch

2 boneless skinless chicken breasts, cut into 1/4-inch-wide strips

1/4 cup soy sauce

1/2 teaspoon bottled minced garlic

1 (8-ounce) bag broccoli slaw mix

1 cup shredded carrots

1 tablespoon dark sesame oil

8 (8-inch) flour tortillas

4 to 8 teaspoons hoisin sauce or plum sauce, or to taste

Heat the peanut oil in a 12-inch nonstick skillet over medium heat. Add the scallions, cabbage and mushrooms. Increase the heat to high and sauté until the vegetables are tender. Combine the sherry and cornstarch in a jar with a tight-fitting lid. Shake to mix well. Add to the skillet. Stir in the chicken, soy sauce and garlic. Stir in the broccoli slaw and carrots. Sauté for 5 to 7 minutes or until the chicken is cooked through. Stir in the sesame oil. Place the tortillas on a microwave-safe plate and cover with waxed paper. Microwave on High for 90 seconds. Spread hoisin sauce on each tortilla and top each with 1/2 cup of the chicken mixture. Roll up, burrito-style, with 1 end tucked in and serve immediately. **Serves 4.**

Note: You may substitute lettuce leaves for the tortillas.

Thai Chicken with Spicy Peanut Sauce

2¹/2 cups water

2¹/2 cups instant rice

2 teaspoons vegetable oil

4 boneless skinless chicken breasts,
    cut into ¹/2-inch strips
    (about 1¹/2 pounds)

1 tablespoon bottled minced garlic

1 tablespoon bottled minced
    ginger

³/4 cup chopped scallions or
    green onions

1 (8-ounce) can sliced bamboo shoots,
    drained

¹/3 cup unsalted peanuts, chopped

1 tablespoon soy sauce

1 tablespoon dry sherry

1 teaspoon sugar

Peanut Sauce (below)

Bring the water to a boil in a 2-quart saucepan. Add the rice and cover. Remove from the heat and let stand until ready to serve. Heat the oil in a 12-inch nonstick skillet over high heat. Add the chicken, garlic and ginger. Sauté for 5 to 7 minutes or until the chicken is cooked through. Stir in the scallions, bamboo shoots, peanuts, soy sauce, sherry and sugar. Stir in the Peanut Sauce. Cook for 2 minutes or until heated through, stirring often. Serve over the rice. **Serves 4.**

Peanut Sauce

2 tablespoons vegetable oil

2 tablespoons soy sauce

2 tablespoons sugar

1¹/2 tablespoons creamy peanut butter

2 teaspoons rice wine vinegar or
    white vinegar

¹/2 teaspoon dark sesame oil

¹/8 teaspoon cayenne pepper

Whisk the vegetable oil, soy sauce, sugar, peanut butter, vinegar, sesame oil and cayenne pepper in a small bowl.

Note: The Peanut Sauce makes an excellent dipping sauce for grilled chicken or pork.

Chicken Enchiladas

1 (4-ounce) can chopped green chiles

3/4 cup loosely packed fresh cilantro leaves and stems

3 green onions, sliced

2 tablespoons sliced pickled jalapeño chiles

2 tablespoons fresh lime juice

1/4 teaspoon salt

1/3 cup water

4 (8-inch) flour tortillas

8 ounces cooked chicken, shredded or cubed

1/4 cup heavy cream

3 ounces Monterey Jack cheese, shredded

Purée the green chiles, cilantro, green onions, jalapeños, lime juice, salt and water in a blender. Pour into an 8-inch skillet. Bring to a boil over medium heat. Boil for 2 minutes. Remove from the heat. Dip 1 side of each tortilla into the sauce and place, sauce side down, on a work surface. Spread 1 tablespoon of sauce on each tortilla. Top with the chicken. Roll up the tortillas and arrange in a greased 7×11-inch baking dish. Stir the cream into the remaining sauce in the skillet. Pour over the tortillas. Cover with foil and bake at 350 degrees for 15 minutes. Sprinkle with the cheese. Bake, uncovered, until the cheese melts. **Serves 4.**

Chicken and Black Bean Enchiladas

3 slices bacon

12 ounces boneless skinless chicken
breasts, cut into short thin strips

2 garlic cloves, minced

1/2 cup picante sauce

1 (16-ounce) can black beans

1 large red bell pepper, chopped

1 teaspoon cumin

1/4 teaspoon salt

1/2 cup sliced green onions

12 flour tortillas

1 1/2 cups shredded Monterey Jack
cheese

1 cup picante sauce

Shredded lettuce

Chopped tomatoes

Sliced avocado

Sour cream

Cook the bacon in a large skillet until crisp. Remove to paper towels to drain; crumble. Remove all but 2 tablespoons of the bacon drippings from the skillet. Add the chicken and garlic and sauté until the chicken is cooked through. Stir in 1/2 cup picante sauce, the black beans, bell pepper, cumin and salt. Simmer for 7 to 8 minutes or until thickened, stirring occasionally. Stir in the green onions and cooked bacon. Place the tortillas on a work surface. Spoon 1/4 cup of the bean mixture down the center of each tortilla. Top each with 1 tablespoon of the cheese. Roll up and place, seam side down, in a greased 9×13-inch baking dish. Spoon 1 cup picante sauce over the tortillas. Bake at 350 degrees for 15 minutes. Sprinkle with the remaining cheese and bake for 5 minutes longer. Serve topped with shredded lettuce, chopped tomatoes, sliced avocado and sour cream. **Serves 4.**

Jalapeño Chicken

1 cup uncooked rice

1 tablespoon butter

2 cups chopped white onions

4 green onion tops, chopped

1 (10-ounce) package frozen chopped spinach,
   cooked and drained

6 jalapeño chiles, chopped, or 3 tablespoons sliced
   pickled jalapeño chiles

3 cups sour cream

2 (10^3/4-ounce) cans condensed cream of chicken soup

^{1}/2 teaspoon salt

4 (2-ounce) packages Doritos, crushed

4 to 6 cups chopped cooked chicken breasts

2^1/2 cups shredded Monterey Jack cheese

Cook the rice using the package directions. Set aside. Melt the butter in a large
saucepan. Add the white onions and green onions and sauté until tender. Remove
from the heat and stir in the spinach, jalapeños, sour cream, soup, rice and salt. Spread
3 of the packages of crushed Doritos in a 9×13-inch baking dish. Sprinkle with
^{1}/2 of the chicken and spread with ^{1}/2 of the spinach mixture. Sprinkle with ^{1}/2 of the
cheese. Top with the remaining chicken and spread with the remaining spinach
mixture. Top with the remaining cheese and sprinkle with the remaining bag of
crushed Doritos. Bake at 350 degrees for 30 to 40 minutes. **Serves 10.**

Skewered Lime Chicken Tenders with Black Bean Sauce

1/2 cup fresh lime juice

1/4 cup fresh orange juice

1/4 cup tequila

1/2 cup chopped fresh cilantro

4 garlic cloves, minced

2 jalapeño chiles, chopped

1 teaspoon chili powder

1/2 teaspoon cumin

11/2 pounds chicken tenders

Salt and pepper to taste

Black Bean Sauce (below)

Mix the lime juice, orange juice, tequila, cilantro, garlic, jalapeños, chili powder and cumin in a 9×13-inch baking dish. Add the chicken and turn to coat. Cover and marinate in the refrigerator for 1 hour, turning occasionally. Remove the chicken and season with salt and pepper. Discard the marinade. Thread the chicken onto wooden skewers that have been soaked in water. Spray the chicken with nonstick cooking spray. Grill over medium-high heat for 8 minutes or until the chicken is cooked through, turning occasionally. Remove to a platter and garnish with chopped cilantro. Serve with Black Bean Sauce. **Serves 12.**

Black Bean Sauce

2 tablespoons minced shallots

1 tablespoon minced garlic

1/4 cup white wine

2 tablespoons sherry

11/2 cups cooked black beans

2 to 3 cups low-fat low-sodium
    chicken broth

1 teaspoon chili powder

1 tablespoon minced fresh cilantro

Salt and pepper to taste

Sauté the shallots and garlic for 1 to 2 minutes in a 2-quart saucepan coated with nonstick cooking spray. Stir in the wine, sherry, black beans and 11/2 cups of the chicken broth. Bring to a simmer and cook for 6 to 8 minutes, stirring often. Remove to a blender or food processor and purée. Return the mixture to the saucepan. Stir in the chili powder and enough of the remaining chicken broth to make the consistency of heavy cream. Cook over medium-low heat until heated through. Stir in the cilantro and season with salt and pepper.

Crescent Pecan Chicken Casserole

1 tablespoon butter

^{1}/2 cup chopped celery

^{1}/2 cup chopped onion

3 cups cubed cooked chicken breasts

1 (10^3/4-ounce) can condensed cream of chicken soup

1 (10^3/4-ounce) can condensed cream of mushroom soup

1 (8-ounce) can water chestnuts, drained and sliced

1 (4-ounce) can sliced mushrooms, drained

^{2}/3 cup mayonnaise

^{1}/2 cup sour cream

^{1}/4 teaspoon curry powder

1 (8-ounce) can refrigerator crescent rolls

1 to 4 tablespoons butter, melted

^{2}/3 cup shredded Cheddar cheese

^{1}/2 cup chopped pecans

Melt 1 tablespoon butter in a large saucepan. Add the celery and onion and sauté until the vegetables are tender. Stir in the chicken, chicken soup, mushroom soup, water chestnuts, mushrooms, mayonnaise, sour cream and curry powder. Cook until heated through; do not boil. Pour into a greased 9×13-inch baking dish. Separate the crescent dough into 2 rectangles. Place on top of the hot chicken mixture. Brush with the melted butter. Sprinkle with the cheese and pecans. Bake at 375 degrees for 20 to 25 minutes or until the crust is a deep golden brown. **Serves 12.**

Simple Chicken or Shrimp Curry

Butter or vegetable oil

1 onion, chopped

4 ounces fresh mushrooms, sliced

$1/2$ teaspoon curry powder

Garlic powder to taste

1 ($10^3/4$-ounce) can condensed cream of mushroom soup

1 cup sour cream

4 chicken breasts, cooked and cubed, or 8 ounces shrimp,
    cooked and peeled

Steamed rice

Chutney

Heat butter in a large saucepan. Add the onion, mushrooms and curry powder. Season with garlic powder. Sauté until the vegetables are tender. Stir in the soup. Simmer for 15 minutes. Stir in the sour cream and chicken. Simmer for 15 minutes. Serve over steamed rice and top with chutney. **Serves 6.**

Grilled Salmon with Ancho Chile Honey Glaze

1 (1-pound) salmon fillet
1 tablespoon olive oil
Juice of 1 lemon
2 garlic cloves, sliced
1 tablespoon chopped fresh basil or dillweed
$1/2$ teaspoon salt
$1/2$ teaspoon pepper, or to taste
Ancho Chile Honey Glaze (below)

Place the salmon in a shallow baking dish. Mix the olive oil, lemon juice, garlic, basil, salt and pepper in a small bowl. Pour over the salmon. Cover and marinate in the refrigerator for 1 to 3 hours. Grill the salmon over medium-hot coals for 5 minutes per side or until the fish flakes easily. Brush with Ancho Chile Honey Glaze. **Serves 2.**

Ancho Chile Honey Glaze

$1/2$ cup honey
2 tablespoons Dijon mustard
2 tablespoons ancho chile powder
Salt and pepper to taste

Whisk the honey, mustard and ancho chile powder in a small bowl. Season with salt and pepper. Store in the refrigerator for up to 2 weeks.

Neskowin Salmon

1 full salmon fillet
6 tablespoons honey
6 tablespoons lime juice
1/4 cup olive oil
Salt and pepper to taste
3/4 cup finely chopped sweet onion
Assorted herbs, such as fennel, thyme, rosemary or
    dillweed (optional)

Place the salmon, skin side down, in a greased baking dish. Tuck the tail under to make
a uniform thickness. Whisk the honey, lime juice and olive oil in a small bowl. Pour
over the salmon. Season with salt and pepper. Sprinkle the onion and herbs over the
salmon. Cover with foil and marinate in the refrigerator for at least 30 minutes. Spoon
the marinade over the salmon. Bake at 425 degrees for 25 to 30 minutes or until the fish
flakes easily. **Serves 8.**

Crispy Lemon Garlic Fish Fillets

1 pound sole, tilapia or flounder
    fillets
1 teaspoon crushed garlic
$1/2$ teaspoon grated lemon zest
Salt and pepper to taste
1 cup rice flour

1 tablespoon chopped fresh parsley
$1/4$ teaspoon cayenne pepper
1 cup milk
$1/2$ cup peanut oil, grapeseed oil or
    other high-quality oil
Freshly squeezed lemon juice

Sprinkle the fish with the garlic and lemon zest. Season with salt and pepper. Mix the rice flour, parsley and cayenne pepper in a shallow dish. Season with salt and pepper. Pour the milk into a shallow dish. Dredge the fish in the flour mixture, then dip in the milk and then dredge in the flour mixture again. Heat the oil in a skillet. Fry the fillets for 8 minutes or until the fish flakes easily. Season with lemon juice. **Serves 4.**

Parmesan Baked Fish Fillets

4 sole, tilapia or orange roughy fillets
Juice of 1 large lemon
Salt and pepper to taste
1 cup mayonnaise

5 tablespoons grated Parmesan cheese
3 tablespoons chopped fresh parsley
1 tablespoon chopped fresh chives
2 egg whites, stiffly beaten

Place the fish in a baking dish and sprinkle with the lemon juice. Cover and chill for 30 minutes. Season lightly with salt and pepper. Mix the mayonnaise, cheese, parsley and chives in a bowl. Fold in the egg whites. Spread over the fish. Cover the dish with foil but do not let it touch the topping. Broil for 10 minutes. Remove the foil and broil until golden brown and the fish flakes easily. **Serves 4.**

Tilapia Gratinée

8 small tilapia fillets

Salt and pepper to taste

1 cup dry vermouth

3 tablespoons butter

3 tablespoons all-purpose flour

$^1/_2$ cup half-and-half

$^1/_4$ cup dry vermouth

2 tomatoes, sliced

4 slices Swiss cheese, halved, or

   $^2/_3$ cup shredded Swiss cheese

2 tablespoons chopped fresh parsley

Arrange the fish in a 9×13-inch baking dish. Season with salt and pepper. Pour 1 cup vermouth over the fish. Bake at 350 degrees for 20 minutes or until the fish flakes easily. Remove the fish to a shallow baking pan. Cover with foil and keep warm. Remove the poaching liquid to a saucepan. Whisk in the butter and flour. Simmer until thick, whisking constantly. Stir in the half-and-half and $^1/_4$ cup vermouth. Cook until the mixture coats the back of a spoon. Arrange the tomato slices on the fish. Pour the sauce over the tomatoes and top with the cheese. Sprinkle with the parsley. Broil for 4 to 6 minutes or until the cheese melts. Serve immediately. **Serves 4.**

Note: This recipe also works well with sole fillets.

Halibut with Artichokes

2 halibut fillets

Salt and pepper to taste

2 tablespoons olive oil

1 garlic clove, minced

1 cup fresh mushrooms, sliced

1 cup canned artichokes

$^1/_2$ cup dry white wine

2 tablespoons capers

Juice of $^1/_2$ lemon

$^1/_8$ teaspoon basil

Season the fish with salt and pepper. Heat the olive oil in a skillet. Add the fish and lightly brown. Remove the fish to a plate. Add the garlic and mushrooms to the skillet. Sauté until the vegetables are tender. Stir in the artichokes, wine and capers. Add the fish. Cook, covered, until the fish flakes easily. Sprinkle with the lemon juice and basil and serve immediately. **Serves 2.**

Crab Cakes with Caper Sauce

1/3 cup mayonnaise
1/3 cup finely chopped green or red
    bell pepper
3 tablespoons finely chopped
    green onions
1 tablespoon fresh lemon juice
1 egg
1 tablespoon chopped fresh parsley

1 tablespoon grainy mustard
1/2 teaspoon salt
1/4 teaspoon cayenne pepper
1 pound cooked fresh lump crab meat
2 slices firm white bread
1/2 cup dry bread crumbs
Olive oil for frying
Caper Sauce (below)

Combine the mayonnaise, bell pepper, green onions, lemon juice, egg, parsley, mustard, salt and cayenne pepper in a bowl. Stir to mix well. Fold in the crab meat gently. Pulse the bread in a food processor to make fine crumbs. Fold into the crab mixture. Cover and chill for 2 hours. Spread 1/2 cup dry bread crumbs in a shallow dish. Fill a 1/2-cup measuring cup loosely with the crab mixture. Turn out onto the bread crumbs. Press gently to form a 1×3-inch patty and coat all sides with bread crumbs. Repeat with the remaining crab mixture. Heat olive oil in a large nonstick skillet over medium-high heat. Add the crab cakes and fry for 2 minutes per side or until crisp and golden brown. Remove to a baking sheet. Bake at 350 degrees for 8 to 9 minutes or until heated through. Serve with Caper Sauce. **Makes 6 crab cakes.**

Caper Sauce

1/3 cup mayonnaise
1 teaspoon grated lemon zest
1 teaspoon fresh lemon juice
1 1/2 teaspoons small capers
1/8 teaspoon salt

Combine the mayonnaise, lemon zest, lemon juice, capers and salt in a small bowl. Stir to mix well.

Crab Newburg

1/4 cup (1/2 stick) butter

2 tablespoons all-purpose flour

1 teaspoon nutmeg

1/2 teaspoon salt

1/8 teaspoon cayenne pepper

2 cups half-and-half

3 egg yolks, lightly beaten

1 (6-ounce) package frozen snow crab, thawed

1 1/2 tablespoons dry sherry

Hot cooked rice

Parsley for garnish

Melt the butter in a saucepan. Add the flour, nutmeg, salt and cayenne pepper and stir until smooth. Stir in the half-and-half gradually. Cook over medium heat for 8 to 10 minutes or until slightly thickened, stirring constantly. Stir 1/2 cup of the hot half-and-half mixture gradually into the beaten egg yolks in a small bowl. Return to the saucepan and stir to mix well. Stir in the crab and liquid. Cook for 1 to 2 minutes or until thickened, stirring constantly. Remove from the heat and stir in the sherry. Serve over rice and garnish with parsley. **Serves 2.**

Note: You can use 2 packages of snow crab, or 1 package of snow crab and 1 small can of shrimp.

Seafood Ensemble

4 slices coarse white bread

$3/4$ cup water

2 tablespoons butter

$1/2$ cup chopped celery

$1/2$ cup chopped green bell pepper

$1/2$ cup chopped onion

2 cups crab meat

2 cups peeled cooked medium shrimp

1 ($13^3/4$-ounce) can artichoke hearts, drained well and quartered

1 ($7^1/2$-ounce) can sliced water chestnuts, drained

$2/3$ cup mayonnaise

3 eggs, beaten

8 ounces sharp Cheddar cheese, shredded

1 tablespoon Worcestershire sauce

Juice of 1 lemon

$1/2$ teaspoon Tony Chachere's Seafood Spice

Dash of Tabasco sauce

Soak the bread in the water in a bowl until the liquid is absorbed. Pinch the bread into small pieces. Melt the butter in a small skillet over medium heat. Add the celery, bell pepper and onion and sauté until the vegetables are tender. Remove to a large bowl. Add the bread pieces, crab meat, shrimp, artichokes, water chestnuts, mayonnaise, eggs, cheese, Worcestershire sauce, lemon juice, seafood spice and Tabasco sauce. Stir to mix well. Spoon into a buttered 2-quart baking dish. Bake at 350 degrees for 30 minutes. **Serves 6 to 8.**

Note: This is best made a day ahead. Cover and chill. Reheat before serving.

Crab-Stuffed Shrimp

12 fresh jumbo shrimp

1/4 cup (1/2 stick) butter

1 onion, finely chopped

1/2 green bell pepper, finely chopped

1/2 cup finely chopped celery

1 pound fresh lump crab meat, drained and flaked

3/4 cup saltine crumbs

1/2 cup mayonnaise

1 tablespoon prepared mustard

2 teaspoons Worcestershire sauce

1/8 teaspoon red pepper

1 egg, beaten

Paprika

1/4 cup (1/2 stick) butter, melted

Peel the shrimp, leaving the tails attached. Devein and butterfly the shrimp. Cook the shrimp in a saucepan of boiling water for 1 minute. Drain and arrange in a single layer in a shallow baking pan. Melt 1/4 cup butter in a heavy skillet. Add the onion, bell pepper and celery and sauté until the vegetables are tender. Remove from the heat. Combine the crab meat, saltine crumbs, mayonnaise, mustard, Worcestershire sauce, red pepper and egg in a bowl. Stir gently to mix. Stir in the sautéed vegetables. Top each shrimp with 3 tablespoons of the crab mixture. Sprinkle with paprika and drizzle with 1/4 cup melted butter. Bake at 350 degrees for 20 minutes. Broil for 6 minutes, basting occasionally with the melted butter in the bottom of the pan. **Serves 4.**

Barbecued Shrimp

1 cup (2 sticks) butter

1 cup olive oil

4 teaspoons minced garlic

4 bay leaves

2 teaspoons rosemary

$^1/_2$ teaspoon basil

$^1/_2$ teaspoon oregano

1 tablespoon paprika

1 teaspoon coarsely ground black pepper

$^1/_2$ teaspoon salt

$^1/_2$ teaspoon red pepper

1 teaspoon lemon juice

2 pounds fresh unpeeled shrimp

Mix the butter, olive oil, garlic, bay leaves, rosemary, basil, oregano, paprika, black pepper, salt, red pepper and lemon juice in a large ovenproof saucepan. Bring to a boil over medium heat, stirring occasionally. Remove from the heat and let stand for at least 1 hour. Stir in the shrimp and cook over medium heat for 6 to 8 minutes or until the shrimp turn pink. Bake, uncovered, at 400 degrees for 10 minutes, stirring the shrimp once or twice. Remove and discard the bay leaves. Serve with French bread and a green salad. **Serves 4 to 6.**

Shrimp à la Creole

1½ pounds fresh deveined peeled shrimp

Salt to taste

Black pepper to taste

Cayenne pepper to taste

Chili powder to taste

½ cup vegetable oil

4 garlic cloves, minced

1 cup chopped onion

1 cup chopped celery

½ cup chopped green bell pepper

1 (6-ounce) can tomato paste

1 teaspoon sugar

1 (4- to 6-ounce) can tomato sauce

2 to 3 cups water

Chopped green onion tops and chopped parsley (optional)

Butterfly the shrimp and arrange on a large platter. Season with salt, black pepper, cayenne pepper and chili powder. Heat the oil in a heavy saucepan over medium heat. Add the garlic, onion, celery and bell pepper and sauté until the vegetables are tender. Add the tomato paste and sugar. Cook for 5 minutes, stirring constantly. Stir in the tomato sauce and 2 cups of the water. Simmer for 40 minutes, stirring frequently. Add more water as needed. Stir in the shrimp. Season with salt, black pepper, cayenne pepper and chili powder. Simmer for 30 minutes or until the shrimp turn pink. Garnish with green onion tops and parsley. **Serves 4.**

Garlicky Rosemary Shrimp

1/4 cup high-quality olive oil

1 large (or more) garlic bulb, peeled and separated into cloves

1 pound fresh unpeeled medium shrimp, rinsed and patted dry

3 bay leaves

1 heaping teaspoon oregano

2 heaping tablespoons chopped fresh rosemary

1/2 teaspoon (or more) crushed red pepper

Salt and freshly ground black pepper to taste

1/2 cup dry white wine

1 tablespoon white wine vinegar

Juice of 1 lemon

Freshly grated nutmeg

Lemon slices

Heat the olive oil in a 12-inch cast-iron skillet over medium heat. Add the garlic and sauté for 2 minutes; do not let brown. Add the shrimp and bay leaves and sauté. Stir in the oregano, rosemary and crushed red pepper. Season with salt and black pepper. Stir in the wine, vinegar and lemon juice. Simmer for 5 minutes or until the shrimp turn pink and the garlic is slightly softened; do not overcook. Remove the bay leaves. Adjust the seasonings to taste and sprinkle generously with nutmeg. Serve in bowls and garnish with lemon slices. **Serves 4.**

Note: This is also wonderful tossed with spinach fettuccini, butter and freshly grated Parmesan cheese, or served at room temperature the next day.

Shrimp and Asparagus au Gratin

4 cups soft bread crumbs

1 cup shredded sharp Cheddar cheese

1/4 cup (1/2 stick) butter or margarine, melted

1 bunch asparagus, cut into 1- to 1 1/2-inch pieces and
    steamed for 10 minutes

1/4 cup (1/2 stick) butter or margarine

1/2 cup all-purpose flour

2 teaspoons salt

1/4 teaspoon pepper

1/2 teaspoon Tony Chachere's Creole Seasoning

3 cups milk

4 cups peeled cooked salad shrimp

Mix the bread crumbs, cheese and 1/4 cup melted butter in a bowl. Spread 1/2 of the bread crumb mixture in a 9×13-inch baking dish. Arrange the asparagus on top. Melt 1/4 cup butter in a saucepan. Stir in the flour, salt, pepper and Creole seasoning. Stir in the milk. Cook until thickened, stirring occasionally. Stir in the shrimp. Pour over the asparagus. Sprinkle with the remaining bread crumb mixture. Bake at 350 degrees for 30 minutes or until golden brown. **Serves 8.**

Note: This is excellent for brunch when paired with Awesome Layered Grits (page 49).

Fettuccini with Shrimp, Tomatoes and Basil

$^1/_2$ cup olive oil

1 pound fresh deveined peeled medium shrimp

4 large ripe tomatoes, seeded and coarsely chopped

$^1/_2$ cup chopped fresh basil

$^1/_3$ cup sliced black olives

3 garlic cloves, minced

2 tablespoons minced shallots

Salt and freshly ground pepper to taste

16 ounces fettuccini, cooked al dente and drained

Grated Romano cheese

Heat the olive oil in a large heavy skillet over medium-high heat. Add the shrimp, tomatoes, basil, olives, garlic and shallots. Season with salt and pepper. Sauté until the shrimp turn pink. Pour over the hot fettuccini in a large bowl. Toss to mix and sprinkle with cheese. Serve immediately. **Serves 4.**

Penne with Vodka Sauce

3 tablespoons butter

1 onion, finely chopped

2 large garlic cloves, minced

1 (28-ounce) can whole plum tomatoes, lightly drained and chopped

1/4 cup vodka

1/4 teaspoon red pepper flakes

1/2 cup heavy cream

12 fresh basil leaves, chopped

Salt and pepper to taste

16 ounces penne pasta, cooked al dente and drained

Freshly grated Parmesan cheese

Chopped fresh basil

Melt the butter in a large skillet over medium heat. Add the onion and cook for 5 minutes, stirring constantly. Add the garlic and cook for 1 minute or just until starting to brown, stirring constantly. Stir in the tomatoes, vodka and red pepper flakes. Simmer for 10 minutes. Stir in the cream and cook until heated through. Stir in the basil and season with salt and pepper. Add the pasta and toss to mix. Serve very hot and top with freshly grated Parmesan cheese and chopped fresh basil, if desired. **Serves 6.**

Cranberry Salsa

1 tablespoon olive oil
1 small onion, chopped
2 tablespoons water
1 (12-ounce) bag fresh cranberries
$^3/4$ cup packed brown sugar
$^1/4$ teaspoon salt
1 (8-ounce) can pineapple, drained and chopped
1 (4-ounce) can chopped green chiles, drained

Heat the olive oil in a saucepan. Add the onion and sauté until tender. Stir in the water, cranberries, brown sugar and salt. Cook until the cranberries pop, stirring occasionally. Remove from the heat and stir in the pineapple and green chiles. Remove to a bowl. Cover and chill. Serve chilled with pork or poultry. **Makes 4 cups.**

Curried Ham Sauce

3 onions
$1^1/2$ cups packed brown sugar
1 (14-ounce) bottle ketchup
$1^3/4$ cups vinegar
$1^1/2$ teaspoons curry powder
1 teaspoon salt
$^1/2$ teaspoon red pepper

Cover the onions with water in a saucepan. Bring to a boil and boil for 5 to 10 minutes. Drain and chop the onions. Return to the saucepan. Stir in the brown sugar, ketchup, vinegar, curry powder, salt and red pepper. Simmer for 30 minutes. **Makes 4 cups.**

"*Vegetarian—that's an old Indian word meaning lousy hunter.*"

—Andy Rooney

Vegetables & Sides

Fresh Asparagus with Parmesan

1 tablespoon balsamic vinegar
1 teaspoon olive oil
1 teaspoon Dijon mustard
1 pound fresh asparagus spears, rinsed
1 teaspoon salt
2 tablespoons grated or shaved fresh Parmesan cheese

Whisk the vinegar, olive oil and mustard in a shallow bowl. Snap off the tough ends of the asparagus spears. Heat 2 inches of water and $1/2$ teaspoon of the salt to boiling in a large skillet. Add $1/2$ of the asparagus. Boil, covered, for 4 to 6 minutes or until tender-crisp. Drain and add to the vinegar mixture. Repeat with the remaining $1/2$ teaspoon salt and the asparagus. Toss the asparagus gently to coat. Sprinkle with the cheese and serve. **Serves 4.**

Asian Asparagus

2 pounds fresh asparagus, trimmed
6 tablespoons soy sauce
$1^1/2$ teaspoons honey
1 tablespoon sesame oil
3 tablespoons toasted sesame seeds

Cook the asparagus in a saucepan of boiling water until tender-crisp. Drain and plunge into ice water to stop the cooking process; drain well. Whisk the soy sauce, honey, sesame oil and sesame seeds in a shallow bowl. Add the asparagus and toss gently to coat. Cover and chill. **Serves 4 to 6.**

Carrot Soufflé

1 pound baby carrots, cooked until very tender and drained

$1/2$ cup (1 stick) butter, melted

3 eggs

$1/2$ cup sugar

3 tablespoons all-purpose flour

1 teaspoon baking powder

1 teaspoon vanilla extract

Purée the carrots and melted butter in a food processor fitted with a metal blade, stopping to scrape down the side as needed. Add the eggs, sugar, flour, baking powder and vanilla. Process until well mixed. Pour into a greased 1-quart baking dish. Bake at 350 degrees for 40 to 45 minutes or until the center is firm. **Serves 4 to 6.**

Seasoned Cauliflower

2 heads cauliflower, cut into florets
3 tablespoons butter
2 tablespoons all-purpose flour
1 1/2 cups milk or half-and-half
1 bay leaf
Generous pinch of nutmeg
2 tablespoons Dijon mustard
1 tablespoon Worcestershire sauce
Salt and pepper to taste
3/4 cup soft white bread crumbs
3 tablespoons butter, melted

Cook the cauliflower in a large saucepan of boiling water for 5 minutes or until tender-crisp. Drain and rinse under cold water; drain well. Melt 3 tablespoons butter in a small heavy saucepan over low heat. Stir in the flour. Cook for 5 minutes, stirring constantly. Whisk in the milk gradually. Stir in the bay leaf and nutmeg. Bring to a simmer, stirring often. Cook, partially covered, for 5 minutes or until thick, stirring often. Stir in the mustard and Worcestershire sauce. Season with salt and pepper. Remove and discard the bay leaf. Pour the sauce into a large bowl. Add the cauliflower and stir to mix. Pour into a 9×13-inch baking pan. Sprinkle with the bread crumbs and drizzle with 3 tablespoons melted butter. Bake at 350 degrees for 45 minutes or until heated through and the edges are bubbly. Place under a broiler for 2 minutes or until golden brown. Remove to a wire rack and let cool for 5 minutes before serving. **Serves 10.**

Note: This can be made 1 day ahead before baking. Cover and chill.

Cream Cheese Corn Casserole

3 (11-ounce) cans white Shoe Peg corn, drained

8 ounces cream cheese, softened

1/2 cup (1 stick) butter, melted

1 (4-ounce) can chopped green chiles

Combine the corn, cream cheese, melted butter and green chiles in a large bowl. Stir to mix well. Pour into a 9×13-inch baking dish. Bake at 350 degrees for 25 to 30 minutes or until heated through. **Serves 6 to 8.**

Corn Zucchini Casserole

2 pounds cooked sliced zucchini

2 eggs, beaten

1 (15 1/4-ounce) can whole kernel corn, drained

1 teaspoon grated onion

8 ounces sharp Cheddar cheese, shredded

Combine the zucchini, eggs, corn, onion and 1/2 of the cheese in a bowl. Stir to mix well. Pour into a greased casserole. Sprinkle with the remaining cheese. Bake at 350 degrees for 30 to 40 minutes. **Serves 6.**

Hominy Casserole

4 (15-ounce) cans hominy, drained

2 (4-ounce) cans chopped green chiles

3 cups sour cream

8 ounces Monterey Jack cheese, shredded

1^1/$_3$ cups finely chopped onions

1 to 2 jalapeño chiles, seeded and chopped

^{1}/$_4$ cup dry bread crumbs

^{1}/$_4$ cup (^{1}/$_2$ stick) butter, cut into small pieces

Chopped pimento (optional)

Combine the hominy, green chiles, sour cream, cheese, onions and jalapeños in a large bowl. Stir to mix well. Spoon into a lightly greased 9×13-inch baking dish. Sprinkle with the bread crumbs and dot with the butter. Bake at 350 degrees for 30 minutes. Sprinkle with pimento. **Serves 16 to 20.**

Green Beans and Artichoke Casserole

1/4 cup olive oil
1 garlic clove, minced
2/3 cup finely chopped onion
1/2 cup Italian-style seasoned
  bread crumbs
1 (14-ounce) can artichoke hearts,
  drained and quartered

1 (10-ounce) package frozen French-
  style green beans, cooked and
  drained
1/2 cup freshly grated Romano cheese
Salt and pepper to taste

Heat the olive oil in a large skillet. Add the garlic and onion and sauté until tender. Add the bread crumbs and stir until the olive oil is absorbed. Stir in the artichokes, green beans and cheese. Season with salt and pepper. Cook until heated through. **Serves 4.**

Guest Green Beans

1/2 cup (1 stick) butter
1 cup packed brown sugar
1/4 teaspoon garlic salt

8 slices bacon
1 pound fresh green beans, trimmed

Melt the butter in a saucepan. Stir in the brown sugar and garlic salt. Bring to a simmer, stirring often. Remove from the heat. Arrange 4 of the bacon slices on a microwave-safe plate. Microwave on High for 2 minutes. Remove to paper towels to drain. Repeat with the remaining bacon. Wrap 1 slice of cooled bacon around 6 to 8 green beans. Secure with a wooden pick. Repeat with the remaining bacon and green beans. Arrange in a single layer in a baking dish. Pour the brown sugar mixture evenly over the beans. Cover with foil. Bake at 350 degrees for 20 to 25 minutes. **Serves 8.**

Note: Fresh asparagus spears may be substituted for the green beans.

French Green Bean Casserole

2 cups sour cream
6 tablespoons sugar
6 heaping tablespoons all-purpose
  flour
2 teaspoons salt
2 tablespoons plus 2 teaspoons
  grated onion

1 (12-ounce) package shredded
  Swiss cheese
3 (8-ounce) packages frozen French-
  style green beans, cooked and
  drained
1 1/2 cups cornflake crumbs
3 to 4 tablespoons butter, melted

Mix the sour cream and sugar in a large saucepan. Add the flour and stir to mix well. Stir in the salt and onion. Add the cheese and stir to mix well. Cook until the cheese melts, stirring often. Add the green beans and stir to mix well. Pour into a 9×13-inch baking dish. Mix the cornflake crumbs and melted butter in a bowl. Sprinkle over the green bean mixture. Bake at 350 degrees for 20 to 30 minutes. **Serves 10.**

Barbecued Beans, Kansas City-Style

2 (16-ounce) cans baked beans
1 cup canned tomatoes, drained
3/4 cup apple juice
1/2 cup ketchup
1/2 cup packed brown sugar
1/2 onion, chopped

1 tablespoon Worcestershire sauce
1 teaspoon seasoned salt
1 teaspoon dry mustard
1/2 teaspoon pepper
2 tablespoons horseradish (optional)

Mix the beans, tomatoes, apple juice, ketchup, brown sugar, onion, Worcestershire sauce, seasoned salt, dry mustard, pepper and horseradish in a shallow 3-quart baking dish. Bake, uncovered, at 350 degrees for 1 1/2 to 2 hours or until the sauce thickens. **Serves 12.**

Baked Spinach with Creamed Vegetable Sauce

2 (10-ounce) packages frozen chopped spinach, cooked and drained
$1/2$ cup bread crumbs
$1/2$ teaspoon salt
$1/8$ teaspoon pepper
$1/2$ cup milk
2 eggs, beaten
$3/4$ cup slivered almonds
$51/3$ tablespoons butter, melted
Creamed Vegetable Sauce (below)

Combine the spinach, bread crumbs, salt, pepper, milk, eggs, almonds and melted butter in a bowl. Stir to mix well. Pack into a buttered 1-quart baking dish. Bake at 325 degrees for 45 minutes or until set. Unmold onto a platter. Top with the Creamed Vegetable Sauce and garnish with carrot slices and parsley sprigs, if desired. **Serves 8.**

Creamed Vegetable Sauce

$1/4$ cup ($1/2$ stick) butter
$1/3$ cup chopped onion
$1/4$ cup all-purpose flour
2 cups milk
$1/2$ cup cooked diced carrots
$1/2$ cup cooked green peas
$1/2$ cup cooked diced celery

Melt the butter in a saucepan. Add the onion and sauté until tender but not brown. Stir in the flour. Stir in the milk gradually. Cook until thickened, stirring constantly. Stir in the carrots, peas and celery and cook until heated through.

Spinach Casserole

1 (16-ounce) carton small curd
    cottage cheese
$1/2$ cup (1 stick) butter
8 ounces Velveeta cheese, cut into
    small cubes

5 to 6 tablespoons all-purpose flour
6 eggs, well beaten
1 (10-ounce) package frozen chopped
    spinach, thawed and well drained

Combine the cottage cheese, butter and Velveeta cheese in a saucepan. Cook over low heat until the cheese melts, stirring often. Remove to a bowl and stir in the flour. Add the eggs and spinach. Stir to mix well. Pour into a greased deep 8×8-inch casserole. Let stand for 10 minutes. Bake at 350 degrees for 1 hour. **Serves 6 to 8.**

Spinach Madeleine

2 (10-ounce) packages frozen
    chopped spinach
$1/4$ cup ($1/2$ stick) butter
2 tablespoons all-purpose flour
2 tablespoons chopped onion
$1/2$ cup evaporated milk
$3/4$ teaspoon garlic salt

$3/4$ teaspoon celery salt
$1/2$ teaspoon pepper
1 teaspoon Worcestershire sauce
1 (6-ounce) roll jalapeño cheese,
    cut into small pieces
Salt and red pepper to taste
Bread crumbs (optional)

Cook the spinach according to the package directions. Drain well, reserving $1/2$ cup of the cooking liquid. Melt the butter in a saucepan. Stir in the flour. Cook until smooth but not brown. Add the onion and cook until tender but not brown. Stir in the evaporated milk and reserved cooking liquid gradually. Cook until thick, stirring often. Stir in the garlic salt, celery salt, pepper, Worcestershire sauce and cheese. Season with salt and red pepper. Cook until the cheese melts, stirring constantly. Stir in the spinach. Serve immediately or pour into a baking dish and top with buttered bread crumbs. Bake at 350 degrees for 5 to 10 minutes or until light brown. **Serves 6.**

Note: This freezes well.

Spinach Artichoke Casserole

1 (13³/4-ounce) can artichoke hearts,
   drained and quartered
2 (10-ounce) packages frozen spinach, cooked,
   drained and squeezed dry
8 ounces cream cheese, softened
¹/4 cup (¹/2 stick) butter, softened
1 (8-ounce) can water chestnuts, drained and chopped
Garlic salt to taste
Onion powder to taste
Pepper to taste
³/4 cup (about) Italian-style seasoned bread crumbs
2 tablespoons butter, melted

Spread the artichokes in an 8×8-inch casserole. Mix the spinach, cream cheese ¹/4 cup butter and the water chestnuts in a bowl. Season with garlic salt, onion powder and pepper. Spread over the artichokes. Mix the bread crumbs and 2 tablespoons melted butter in a small bowl. Sprinkle over the spinach mixture. Bake at 350 degrees for 30 minutes. **Serves 6 to 8.**

Note: This can be made ahead. Cover and chill. Bake just before serving.

Summer Squash Casserole

2 cups water

2 pounds yellow summer squash, sliced (about 6 cups)

1/4 cup chopped onion

1 (10 3/4-ounce) can condensed cream of chicken soup

1 cup sour cream

1 cup shredded carrots

1 (8-ounce) package herb-seasoned stuffing mix

1/2 cup (1 stick) butter, melted

Bring the water to a boil in a saucepan. Add the squash and onion. Cook for 5 minutes; drain well. Mix the soup, sour cream and carrots in a bowl. Fold in the squash and onion. Mix the stuffing mix with the melted butter in a bowl. Spread 1/2 of the stuffing mix in a 7×12-inch baking dish. Top with the squash mixture. Sprinkle with the remaining stuffing mix. Bake at 350 degrees for 25 to 30 minutes. Let stand for 3 minutes. **Serves 10.**

Squash and Rice Casserole

1/2 cup (1 stick) margarine, softened

1 cup chopped onion

2 (6-ounce) rolls garlic cheese

2 cups cooked rice

8 to 10 squash, cooked and mashed

1 (14-ounce) can chicken broth

1 (4-ounce) can chopped green chiles

1 1/2 teaspoons sugar

Salt and pepper to taste

Combine the margarine, onion, cheese, rice, squash, chicken broth, green chiles and sugar in a large bowl. Season with salt and pepper. Stir to mix well. Pour into a large casserole. Bake at 350 degrees for 30 minutes. **Serves 10.**

Sweet Potato Casserole

3 cups mashed cooked sweet potatoes

1 cup granulated sugar

1/2 cup packed brown sugar

6 tablespoons butter, softened

1 (14-ounce) can sweetened
   condensed milk

3 eggs, beaten

1/2 teaspoon nutmeg

1/2 teaspoon cinnamon

1 teaspoon vanilla extract

6 tablespoons butter, softened

1 cup cornflakes, crushed

1/2 cup packed brown sugar

1/2 cup pecans, chopped

Combine the sweet potatoes, granulated sugar, 1/2 cup brown sugar, 6 tablespoons butter, the sweetened condensed milk, eggs, nutmeg, cinnamon and vanilla in a large bowl. Stir to mix well. Pour into a buttered 9×13-inch baking dish. Bake at 400 degrees for 15 minutes. Combine 6 tablespoons butter, the cornflakes, 1/2 cup brown sugar and pecans in a bowl. Stir to mix well. Spread over the sweet potato mixture. Bake for 15 minutes longer. **Serves 10.**

Bourbon Sweet Potatoes

6 sweet potatoes (about 4 pounds)

1/2 cup (1 stick) butter, softened

1/2 cup packed brown sugar

1/3 cup orange juice

1/4 cup bourbon

1/2 teaspoon salt

1/2 teaspoon pumpkin pie spice

1/2 cup chopped pecans

Cook the sweet potatoes in a saucepan of boiling water for 20 to 25 minutes or until tender. Drain and cool to the touch. Peel and mash in a bowl. Add the butter, brown sugar, orange juice, bourbon, salt and pumpkin pie spice. Stir to mix well. Spoon into a lightly greased 1 1/2-quart baking dish. Sprinkle the pecans around the edge. Bake at 375 degrees for 45 minutes. **Serves 8.**

Red Bliss Garlic Mashed Potatoes

1 cup heavy cream

2 tablespoons butter

2 pounds unpeeled red bliss potatoes,
 rinsed and diced

6 garlic cloves, roasted and mashed

1 tablespoon wasabi paste

Salt and pepper to taste

6 slices extra-thick bacon, crisp-cooked
 and crumbled

Warm the cream and butter in a small saucepan. Cover the potatoes with cold water in
a saucepan. Cover and bring to a boil. Uncover and cook until the potatoes are tender.
Drain well and return to the saucepan. Mash by hand with a potato masher. Stir in the
warm cream mixture gradually. Stir in the garlic and wasabi paste. Season with salt
and pepper. Remove to a serving bowl. Top with the bacon and serve immediately.
Serves 4 to 6.

Three-Cheese Potato Casserole

2 pounds new potatoes

$1/2$ teaspoon salt

$1/2$ teaspoon pepper

$3/4$ teaspoon granulated garlic

2 tablespoons finely chopped
 fresh parsley

3 tablespoons finely chopped onion

2 ounces Swiss cheese, shredded

$2^1/2$ ounces feta cheese, crumbled

$2^1/2$ ounces sharp Cheddar cheese,
 shredded

6 tablespoons butter, melted

Cook the potatoes in a saucepan of boiling water just until tender; do not overcook.
Drain and let cool. Grate the potatoes into a large bowl. Add the salt, pepper, garlic,
parsley, onion, Swiss cheese, feta cheese, Cheddar cheese and melted butter. Stir to
mix well. Spoon into a 9×13-inch baking dish. Bake at 350 degrees for 1 hour.
Serves 8 to 10.

Potato Croquettes

3 large baking potatoes
8 ounces extra-sharp Cheddar cheese, shredded
$1/4$ cup ($1/2$ stick) butter or margarine, softened
$1/2$ cup chopped green onions
$1/4$ cup chopped fresh parsley

1 egg, lightly beaten
1 teaspoon salt
$1/2$ teaspoon black pepper
$1/4$ teaspoon cayenne pepper
2 cups crushed butter crackers (about 1 sleeve)

Bake the potatoes at 350 degrees for 1 hour or until tender. Remove to a wire rack and let cool. Peel and mash in a bowl. Add the cheese, butter, green onions, parsley, egg, salt, black pepper and cayenne pepper. Stir to mix well. Shape $1/2$ cup of the potato mixture into a ball. Roll in the crushed crackers and place on an ungreased baking sheet. Repeat with the remaining potato mixture and crushed crackers. Bake at 350 degrees for 30 to 35 minutes or until golden brown. **Serves 10 to 12.**

Texas Hash

2 ($10^3/4$-ounce) cans condensed cream of chicken and mushroom soup
1 large onion, chopped
8 ounces cream cheese, softened
2 cups sour cream

1 (2-pound) bag frozen hash brown potatoes
1 (8-ounce) package frozen corn
1 cup shredded Cheddar cheese
2 cups crushed bread stuffing mix
$1/2$ cup (1 stick) butter, melted

Combine the soup, onion, cream cheese, sour cream, potatoes and corn in a large bowl. Stir to mix well. Spoon into a greased 9×13-inch baking dish. Sprinkle with the cheese. Mix the stuffing mix with the melted butter in a bowl. Sprinkle over the cheese. Bake at 350 degrees for 45 minutes to 1 hour. **Serves 12.**

Turkey Stuffing

1/2 cup (1 stick) butter

6 celery ribs, chopped

2 onions, chopped

3/4 cup rice

1 (14-ounce) can chicken broth

2 tablespoons butter

1 (8-ounce) package button mushrooms, sliced

2 pounds bulk pork sausage, cooked, drained and crumbled

2/3 (8×8-inch pan) baked corn bread, crumbled

1 (8-ounce) can water chestnuts, drained and quartered

1 (5-ounce) can sliced black olives, drained

1 cup pecans, coarsely chopped

1 1/2 cups herb-seasoned stuffing mix

Chopped fresh parsley (optional)

Chopped fresh sage (optional)

2 eggs, beaten

1 (14-ounce) can chicken broth

Melt 1/2 cup butter in a saucepan. Add the celery and onions and sauté until tender.
Remove to a large bowl. Combine the rice and 1 can chicken broth in a saucepan.
Cook until the rice is tender and the liquid is absorbed. Add to the sautéed vegetables.
Melt 2 tablespoons butter in a skillet over medium-high heat. Add the mushrooms
and sauté for 2 minutes or until tender. Add to the rice mixture. Add the sausage,
corn bread, water chestnuts, olives, pecans and stuffing mix. Season with parsley
and sage. Stir to mix well. Add the eggs and 1 can chicken broth. Stir to mix well.
Makes enough to stuff a 16-pound turkey.

Note: Can be partially prepared a day ahead. Cover and chill. Mix in the eggs and
1 can chicken broth when ready to stuff the turkey.

Mexican Dressing

8 slices bacon, chopped

6 ounces venison sausage or medium-hot bulk pork sausage

1/2 cup chopped poblano chile

2 serrano chiles, seeded and chopped

1 garlic clove, minced

1 red bell pepper, chopped

1 yellow bell pepper, chopped

1 orange bell pepper, chopped

2 celery ribs, chopped

1/4 cup chopped Spanish onion

Handful fresh cilantro, chopped

2 small baguettes, or 4 slices white sandwich bread, cubed

1 cup crumbled corn bread

2 cups chicken stock

1 egg, beaten

Cook the bacon and sausage in a large saucepan until the sausage is crumbly and cooked through and the bacon is crisp. Do not drain. Add the poblano chile, serrano chiles, garlic, red bell pepper, yellow bell pepper, orange bell pepper, celery and onion. Sauté for 8 to 10 minutes or until the vegetables are tender. Add the cilantro, bread cubes, crumbled corn bread and chicken stock. Stir to mix well. Remove to a large bowl. Add the egg and stir to mix well. Pour into a 10×10-inch baking dish. Bake at 375 degrees for 20 minutes. Serve warm. **Serves 12.**

Cilantro Rice

4 tomatillos, husked, rinsed
  and chopped
$1/4$ cup chopped fresh cilantro
2 serrano chiles, seeded and chopped
1 cup water or chicken stock
2 cups rice

6 scallions, chopped
1 large garlic clove, minced
2 teaspoons salt
2 cups water or chicken stock
$1/4$ cup chopped fresh cilantro

Purée the tomatillos, $1/4$ cup cilantro, the serrano chiles and 1 cup water in a blender. Remove to a large saucepan. Stir in the rice, scallions, garlic, salt and 2 cups water. Bring to a boil and stir once with a fork. Reduce the heat. Simmer, covered, for 12 to 15 minutes or until the liquid is absorbed. Fluff the rice with a fork and stir in $1/4$ cup cilantro. Cover and let stand for 5 minutes. Remove to a serving dish. **Serves 8.**

Sesame Noodles

1 tablespoon olive oil
Pinch of salt
32 ounces rotelli pasta
$1/2$ cup sesame oil
$1/2$ cup soy sauce

$1/2$ cup toasted sesame seeds
$1/2$ cup chopped scallions
$1 1/2$ teaspoons garlic powder
$1/4$ to $1/2$ teaspoon cayenne pepper
$1/2$ cup chopped fresh cilantro

Add the olive oil and salt to a large saucepan of boiling water. Add the pasta and cook until al dente. Drain and cool. Remove to a large bowl. Add the sesame oil, soy sauce, sesame seeds, scallions, garlic powder and cayenne pepper. Toss gently to mix. Sprinkle with the cilantro just before serving. **Serves 18.**

Sautéed Mushrooms

2 cups sliced fresh mushrooms
1/2 cup (1 stick) butter
1/4 cup Worcestershire sauce
1/2 cup dry red wine
1 teaspoon minced garlic
Salt and pepper to taste

Combine the mushrooms, butter, Worcestershire sauce, wine and garlic in a saucepan. Season with salt and pepper. Cover and bring to a boil over medium-high heat. Reduce the heat to low and simmer for 30 minutes. **Serves 4 to 6.**

Baked Creamy Mushrooms

1 pound whole mushrooms, rinsed and stems removed
1/2 cup (1 stick) butter
2 tablespoons all-purpose flour
2/3 cup half-and-half
1/2 cup chicken broth
Dash of pepper
1 heaping cup fresh bread crumbs
3/4 cup grated Parmesan cheese

Arrange the mushrooms, stemmed side down, in a shallow 8×11-inch baking dish. Melt the butter in a skillet over low heat. Increase the heat to medium-high and stir in the flour. Cook for 3 minutes, stirring constantly. Stir in the half-and-half gradually. Stir in the chicken broth gradually. Season with pepper. Simmer until thickened, stirring often. Pour over the mushrooms. Sprinkle with the bread crumbs. Bake at 350 degrees for 30 minutes. Sprinkle with the cheese. Bake for 5 minutes longer or until the cheese melts. Serve hot. **Serves 4 to 6.**

Dutch Onion Rings

2 onions, sliced $1/4$ inch thick and separated into rings

$1/2$ cup sour cream

2 teaspoons fresh lemon juice

1 teaspoon celery seeds

$1/2$ teaspoon salt

Cover the onion rings with boiling water in a large bowl. Let stand for 2 minutes. Drain, cover and chill. Mix the sour cream, lemon juice, celery seeds and salt in a small bowl. Add to the onions and toss to mix. Serve immediately. **Serves 6 to 8.**

Onion Casserole

5 cups boiling water

1/2 cup rice

1/4 cup (1/2 stick) butter

3 pounds sweet onions, chopped (about 7^1/2 cups)

8 ounces Swiss cheese, shredded

Dash of salt

3/4 cup (or more) half-and-half

Combine the boiling water and rice in a saucepan. Cook, covered, for 5 minutes. Drain and set aside. Melt the butter in a large heavy skillet over medium-high heat. Add the onions and sauté until tender. Remove from the heat and add the rice, cheese, salt and 2/3 cup of the half-and-half. Stir to mix well. Pour into a 1^1/2-quart casserole coated with nonstick cooking spray. Add the remaining half-and-half, adding more if needed for the half-and-half to be visible at the edges. Bake, covered, at 300 degrees for 1 hour. Serve warm. **Serves 12.**

"Vegetables are a must on a diet.
I suggest carrot cake, zucchini
bread, and pumpkin pie."

—Jim Davis, "Garfield"

Decadent Desserts

Amaretto Cake

1 (2-layer) package yellow cake mix
1 (3¹/₂-ounce) package vanilla instant
   pudding mix
4 eggs
¹/₂ cup vegetable oil

³/₄ cup amaretto
¹/₂ cup water
¹/₄ teaspoon almond extract
1 cup confectioners' sugar
6 tablespoons amaretto

Combine the cake mix, pudding mix, eggs, oil, ³/₄ cup amaretto, the water and almond extract in a large bowl. Beat to mix well. Pour into a greased and floured bundt pan. Bake at 350 degrees for 45 to 50 minutes or until a wooden pick inserted in the center comes out clean. Remove to a wire rack. Poke holes in the top of the cake with a fork. Mix the confectioners' sugar and 6 tablespoons amaretto in a bowl until smooth. Pour over the warm cake. Let the cake cool in the pan. **Serves 10 to 12.**

Blackberry Wine Cake

1 cup chopped walnuts
1 (2-layer) package yellow cake mix
¹/₂ cup vegetable oil
1 cup blackberry wine
4 eggs

1 (3-ounce) package black cherry or
   blackberry gelatin
1 cup confectioners' sugar
1 teaspoon vegetable oil
¹/₄ cup (or more) blackberry wine

Sprinkle the walnuts evenly in the bottom of a greased and floured bundt pan. Combine the cake mix, oil, 1 cup wine, the eggs and gelatin in a large bowl. Beat with an electric mixer at low speed until moistened. Beat at medium speed for 2 minutes. Pour into the prepared bundt pan. Bake at 350 degrees for 45 minutes or until a wooden pick inserted in the center comes out clean. Remove to a wire rack. Poke holes in the top of the cake with a fork. Mix the confectioners' sugar, oil and ¹/₄ cup wine in a bowl until the sugar dissolves. Add more wine if needed to make a drizzling consistency. Pour over the hot cake. Let the cake cool in the pan. **Serves 12.**

Totally Divine Carrot Cake

3 cups unbleached all-purpose flour

3 cups sugar

1 teaspoon salt

1 tablespoon baking soda

1 tablespoon cinnamon

$1^1/2$ cups corn oil

4 eggs, lightly beaten

1 tablespoon vanilla extract

$1^1/2$ cups walnuts, chopped

$1^1/2$ cups flaked coconut

$1^1/3$ cups puréed cooked carrots

$3/4$ cup drained crushed pineapple

Cream Cheese Frosting (below)

$1/2$ cup finely chopped walnuts

Walnut halves

Sift the flour, sugar, salt, baking soda and cinnamon into a large bowl. Add the oil, eggs and vanilla. Beat to mix well. Fold in $1^1/2$ cups walnuts, the coconut, carrots and pineapple. Pour into 2 greased 9-inch cake pans lined with waxed paper. Bake at 350 degrees on the middle rack for 30 to 35 minutes or until a wooden pick inserted in the center comes out clean and the edges of the layers are pulling away from the pan. Remove to a wire rack and cool in the pans for 3 hours. Remove the cake from the pans. Spread the Cream Cheese Frosting between the layers and over the top and side of the cake. Dust the sides of the cake with $1/2$ cup chopped walnuts and decorate the top with walnut halves. **Serves 12.**

Cream Cheese Frosting

6 tablespoons butter, softened

8 ounces cream cheese, softened

3 cups confectioners' sugar, sifted

1 teaspoon vanilla extract

Juice of $1/2$ lemon

Cream the butter and cream cheese in a bowl. Beat in the confectioners' sugar gradually and beat until smooth. Stir in the vanilla and lemon juice.

Chocolate Earthquake Cake

1 1/2 cups chopped pecans

1 (3 1/2-ounce) can flaked coconut

1 (2-layer) package German Chocolate cake mix,
    batter prepared according to the package directions

1/2 cup (1 stick) margarine, melted

8 ounces cream cheese, softened

1 (16-ounce) package confectioners' sugar

Spread the pecans in a greased 9×13-inch baking pan. Sprinkle with the coconut. Pour the batter evenly over the coconut. Beat the melted margarine, cream cheese and confectioners' sugar in a bowl until smooth. Spoon over the batter. Bake at 350 degrees for 45 minutes. Remove to a wire rack to cool. **Serves 12 to 16.**

Italian Cream Cake

2 cups sugar	2 cups sifted all-purpose flour
1/2 cup (1 stick) butter, softened	1 teaspoon vanilla extract
1/2 cup shortening	5 egg whites
5 egg yolks	1 cup chopped pecans
1 cup buttermilk	1 (3 1/2-ounce) can flaked coconut
1 teaspoon baking soda	Cream Cheese Icing (below)

Beat the sugar, butter and shortening in a large bowl until light and fluffy. Add the egg yolks, 1 at a time, beating well after each addition. Mix the buttermilk and baking soda in a small bowl. Beat into the sugar mixture alternately with the flour. Stir in the vanilla. Beat the egg whites in a bowl until stiff peaks form. Fold into the batter. Fold in the pecans and coconut gently. Pour into 3 greased and floured 9-inch cake pans. Bake at 325 degrees for 25 minutes or until a wooden pick inserted in the center comes out clean. Cool in the pans for 10 minutes. Remove to a wire rack to cool completely. Spread the Cream Cheese Icing between the layers and over the top and side of the cake. **Serves 12.**

Cream Cheese Icing

1/2 cup (1 stick) margarine, softened	1 (16-ounce) package confectioners' sugar
8 ounces cream cheese, softened	
1 teaspoon vanilla extract	

Cream the margarine and cream cheese in a bowl. Beat in the vanilla. Beat in the confectioners' sugar and beat until smooth.

Choco-Chip Pound Cake

1 (2-layer) package yellow cake mix
1 ($3^1/_2$-ounce) package vanilla instant
   pudding mix
1 ($3^1/_2$-ounce) package chocolate
   instant pudding mix
4 eggs
$^1/_2$ cup vegetable oil

1 cup water
2 cups semisweet chocolate chips
$^1/_2$ cup sugar
$2^1/_2$ tablespoons milk
$2^1/_2$ tablespoons butter
$^1/_2$ cup semisweet chocolate chips

Combine the cake mix, vanilla pudding mix, chocolate pudding mix, eggs, oil, water and 2 cups chocolate chips in a large bowl. Beat to mix well. Pour into a greased and floured bundt pan. Bake at 350 degrees for 45 to 50 minutes or until a wooden pick inserted in the center comes out clean. Cool in the pan for 10 to 15 minutes. Remove to a wire rack to cool completely. Mix the sugar, milk and butter in a small saucepan. Bring to a boil over medium heat. Remove from the heat and add $^1/_2$ cup chocolate chips. Stir until the chocolate melts. Drizzle over the cake or dust with confectioners' sugar. **Serves 12.**

Lemon Pound Cake

1 (2-layer) package lemon cake mix
1 cup apricot nectar
$^3/_4$ cup vegetable oil
$^1/_2$ cup sugar

4 eggs
$^1/_4$ cup lemon juice
1 cup confectioners' sugar

Beat the cake mix, apricot nectar, oil and sugar in a large bowl. Add the eggs, 1 at a time, beating well after each addition. Pour into a greased and floured tube or bundt pan. Bake at 350 degrees for 30 to 40 minutes or until a wooden pick inserted in the center comes out clean. Cool in the pan for 10 to 15 minutes. Remove to a wire rack to cool completely. Mix the lemon juice and confectioners' sugar in a bowl until smooth. Drizzle over the cake. **Serves 10 to 12.**

Raspberry Cordial Cake

6 ounces frozen whole raspberries

1/4 cup raspberry gelatin powder

1 (2-layer) package white cake mix

1 (4-ounce) package vanilla instant
pudding mix

3/4 cup plus 2 tablespoons water

1/2 cup canola oil

4 eggs

Raspberry Glaze (below)

Heat the raspberries in a saucepan over low heat until beginning to boil. Stir in the gelatin. Boil for a few minutes. Remove from the heat and let cool. Combine the cake mix, pudding mix, water, oil and eggs in a large bowl. Beat with an electric mixer at low speed for 2 minutes. Scrape the bottom and side of the bowl. Beat at medium speed for 1 minute. Remove 1/2 cup batter and stir into the cooled raspberry mixture. Pour 1/2 of the plain batter into a greased and floured bundt pan. Drizzle 3 tablespoons of the raspberry mixture on top. Swirl with a knife. Add the remaining plain batter. Drizzle the remaining raspberry mixture and swirl with a knife. Bake at 350 degrees for 50 minutes or until a wooden pick inserted in the center comes out clean. Remove to a wire rack and let cool slightly. Poke holes in the top of the cake with a fork. Pour the Raspberry Glaze over the warm cake. Let stand for 15 minutes. Remove to a serving plate. Store in an airtight container in the refrigerator. **Serves 12.**

Raspberry Glaze

1/2 cup (1 stick) butter

1 cup sugar

1/4 cup water

1/2 teaspoon raspberry gelatin powder

1/4 cup brandy

1/4 cup raspberry schnapps

Mix the butter, sugar and water in a saucepan. Bring to a boil and boil for 3 minutes. Stir in the gelatin and remove from the heat. Let cool slightly and stir in the brandy and raspberry schnapps.

Rum Cake

   1 cup chopped pecans
   1 (2-layer) package yellow cake mix
   1 (3^{1}/$_{2}$-ounce) package vanilla instant pudding mix
   4 eggs
   ^{1}/$_{2}$ cup vegetable oil
   ^{1}/$_{2}$ cup cold water
   ^{1}/$_{2}$ cup dark rum
   Rum Glaze (below)

Sprinkle the pecans evenly over the bottom of a greased and floured bundt pan.
Combine the cake mix, pudding mix, eggs, oil, water and rum in a large bowl. Beat to
mix well. Pour into the prepared bundt pan. Bake at 325 degrees for 1 hour or until a
wooden pick inserted in the center comes out clean. Cool in the pan for 10 to 15
minutes. Invert onto a serving plate. Poke holes in the top of the cake with a fork.
Drizzle some of the Rum Glaze over the top and side of the hot cake, allowing the cake
to absorb the glaze. Continue drizzling until all of the glaze is used. **Serves 12.**

Rum Glaze

   ^{1}/$_{2}$ cup (1 stick) butter
   ^{1}/$_{4}$ cup water
   1 cup sugar
   ^{1}/$_{2}$ cup dark rum

Melt the butter in a saucepan. Stir in the water and sugar. Bring to a boil and boil for
5 minutes, stirring constantly. Remove from the heat and stir in the rum.

Russian Cake

1 (2-layer) package yellow cake mix

1 (3^{1}/$_{2}$-ounce) package chocolate instant pudding mix

^{1}/$_{2}$ cup sugar

1 cup vegetable oil

4 eggs

^{3}/$_{4}$ cup water

^{1}/$_{4}$ cup vodka

^{1}/$_{4}$ cup Kahlúa

^{1}/$_{2}$ cup confectioners' sugar

^{1}/$_{2}$ cup Kahlúa

Combine the cake mix, pudding mix, sugar, oil, eggs, water, vodka and ^{1}/4 cup Kahlúa in a large bowl. Beat with an electric mixer at low speed for 1 minute. Beat at medium speed for 4 minutes. Pour into a greased and floured bundt pan. Bake at 350 degrees for 50 minutes or until a wooden pick inserted in the center comes out clean. Cool in the pan for 10 to 15 minutes. Invert onto a serving plate. Poke holes in the top of the cake with a wooden pick. Beat the confectioners' sugar and ^{1}/2 cup Kahlúa in a small bowl until smooth. Drizzle over the hot cake. Serve with whipped cream. **Serves 10 to 12.**

Black Bottom Cupcakes

  3 cups all-purpose flour
  2 cups sugar
  $1/4$ cup baking cocoa
  1 teaspoon salt
  2 teaspoons baking soda
  2 cups water
  $2/3$ cup vegetable oil
  2 teaspoons vanilla extract
  2 tablespoons vinegar
  Filling (below)

Mix the flour, sugar, baking cocoa, salt and baking soda in a large bowl. Add the water, oil, vanilla and vinegar and beat until smooth. Place foil liners in muffin cups. Fill prepared muffin cups $1/2$ to $2/3$ full. Spoon 1 teaspoon of the Filling onto each cupcake. Bake at 350 degrees for 20 to 25 minutes. Cool in the pans for 5 minutes. Remove to a wire rack to cool. **Makes 2 dozen cupcakes.**

Filling

  8 ounces cream cheese, softened
  $2/3$ cup sugar
  $1/2$ teaspoon salt
  1 egg
  1 cup chocolate chips

Beat the cream cheese, sugar, salt and egg in a bowl until smooth. Stir in the chocolate chips.

Almond Butter Crunch

1 cup (2 sticks) butter
1¹/3 cups sugar
1 tablespoon light corn syrup
3 tablespoons water
1 cup coarsely chopped blanched
　　almonds, toasted

4 (4-ounce) chocolate candy bars,
　　melted
1 cup finely chopped blanched
　　almonds, toasted

Melt the butter in a large saucepan. Stir in the sugar, corn syrup and water. Cook to 300 degrees on a candy thermometer, hard-crack stage, stirring occasionally. Watch closely so that the mixture does not burn. Remove from the heat and quickly stir in 1 cup coarsely chopped almonds. Pour onto a sheet of buttered foil and let cool. Spread the top of the candy with ¹/2 of the melted chocolate. Sprinkle with ¹/2 of the finely chopped almonds. Cover with waxed paper and invert. Spread the remaining chocolate on the top and sprinkle with the remaining finely chopped almonds. Let cool. Chill to firm the chocolate, if necessary. Break into pieces. **Serves 16.**

Texas Millionaires

1 (14-ounce) package caramels
2 tablespoons water
2 tablespoons butter

2 cups coarsely chopped pecans
2²/3 cups chocolate chips
¹/4 bar paraffin

Combine the caramels and water in a saucepan. Cook until the caramels are melted. Add the butter and stir until melted. Stir in the pecans. Drop by teaspoonfuls onto buttered waxed paper and cool until firm. Melt the chocolate chips and paraffin in the top of a double boiler or in a microwave-safe bowl in the microwave. Dip the candy pieces into the melted chocolate using a wooden pick to hold the candy. Place on buttered waxed paper to firm. **Makes about 40 candies.**

Angel Spiced Pecans

1 egg white
1 tablespoon butter, melted
1 teaspoon vanilla extract
1 pound pecan halves
$1/2$ cup sugar
$1^1/2$ teaspoons cinnamon
Generous pinch of allspice
$1/2$ teaspoon salt

Whisk the egg white in a large bowl until foamy. Stir in the butter and vanilla gently. Add the pecans and stir gently to coat. Mix the sugar, cinnamon, allspice and salt in a small bowl. Sprinkle over the pecans and stir to mix. Spread the pecan mixture on a parchment-lined baking sheet. Bake at 250 degrees for 25 minutes. Stir the pecans. Bake for 25 minutes longer. Remove to a wire rack to cool. Store in an airtight container. **Makes about 2 cups.**

Beacon Hill Cookies

1 cup semisweet chocolate chips
2 egg whites
Dash of salt
$^1/_2$ cup sugar

$^1/_2$ teaspoon vanilla extract
$^1/_2$ teaspoon vinegar
$^3/_4$ cup chopped walnuts

Melt the chocolate chips in the top of a double boiler over hot water. Beat the egg whites and salt in a bowl until foamy. Beat in the sugar gradually. Beat until stiff peaks form. Beat in the vanilla and vinegar. Fold in the melted chocolate and walnuts. Drop by teaspoonfuls onto a greased cookie sheet. Top with additional chopped walnuts, if desired. Bake at 350 degrees for 10 minutes. Remove the cookies to a wire rack to cool. **Makes 3 dozen cookies.**

Delicious Chocolate Chip Cookies

$^1/_2$ cup (1 stick) unsalted butter, softened
1 cup packed brown sugar
3 tablespoons granulated sugar
1 egg
2 teaspoons vanilla extract
$1^3/_4$ cups all-purpose flour

$^1/_2$ teaspoon baking powder
$^1/_2$ teaspoon baking soda
$^1/_2$ teaspoon salt
$1^1/_2$ teaspoons instant coffee granules, slightly crushed
$1^1/_3$ cups semisweet chocolate chips

Beat the butter, brown sugar and granulated sugar in a large bowl until light and fluffy. Beat in the egg and vanilla. Mix the flour, baking powder, baking soda, salt and coffee granules together. Beat into the butter mixture. Stir in the chocolate chips. Drop by large spoonfuls onto a greased cookie sheet. Bake at 375 degrees for 8 to 10 minutes or for 10 to 12 minutes for a crisper cookie. Remove the cookies to a wire rack to cool. **Makes 3 dozen cookies.**

Macaroonies

2 eggs

1/8 teaspoon salt

3/4 cup sugar

1/2 cup all-purpose flour

1 tablespoon butter, melted

2 cups flaked coconut

1 cup semisweet chocolate chips

1 teaspoon grated lemon zest or
    orange zest

1 teaspoon vanilla extract

Beat the eggs and salt in a large bowl until foamy. Beat in the sugar gradually. Beat for 5 to 7 minutes or until thick and ivory-colored. Fold in the flour and melted butter. Stir in the coconut, chocolate chips, lemon zest and vanilla. Drop by rounded teaspoonfuls onto lightly greased and floured cookie sheets. Bake at 325 degrees for 12 to 15 minutes or until light brown. Cool on the cookie sheet for 1 minute. Remove to a wire rack to cool. **Makes about 3 dozen cookies.**

Monster Cookies

1/2 cup (1 stick) margarine, softened

1 cup granulated sugar

1 cup plus 2 tablespoons packed brown
    sugar

3 eggs

2 cups peanut butter

1/4 teaspoon vanilla extract

3/4 teaspoon light corn syrup

4 1/2 cups rolled oats

2 teaspoons baking soda

1/4 teaspoon salt

1 cup "M&M's" Chocolate Candies

1 cup chocolate chips

Beat the margarine in a large bowl until light and fluffy. Beat in the granulated sugar and brown sugar gradually. Add the eggs, peanut butter, vanilla and corn syrup. Beat to mix well. Add the oats, baking soda and salt. Stir to mix well. Stir in the candy and chocolate chips; the dough will be stiff. Drop by 1/4 cupfuls, 4 inches apart, onto a lightly greased cookie sheet. Press each cookie lightly to form a 3 1/2-inch circle. Bake at 350 degrees for 12 to 15 minutes. Cool on the cookie sheet for 1 minute. Remove to a wire rack to cool. **Makes 2 1/2 dozen cookies.**

Pecan Balls

1 cup pecans, finely ground
2 tablespoons sugar
$^1/_2$ cup (1 stick) butter, softened
1 teaspoon vanilla extract
1 cup sifted all-purpose flour
Pinch of salt
Confectioners' sugar

Combine the pecans, sugar, butter, vanilla, flour and salt in a bowl. Work with hands until the mixture holds together. Pinch off pieces of dough and roll into walnut-size balls. Place on an ungreased cookie sheet. Bake at 375 degrees for 20 minutes. Cool on the cookie sheet for 1 minute. Roll the warm pecan balls in confectioners' sugar. **Makes about 2 dozen cookies.**

Meringue-Topped Brownies

1 cup (2 sticks) butter or margarine, softened
1/2 cup packed brown sugar
1/2 cup granulated sugar
3 egg yolks
2 cups sifted all-purpose flour
1/4 teaspoon salt
1/4 teaspoon baking soda
1 tablespoon cold milk
1 tablespoon vanilla extract
1 cup chocolate chips
3 egg whites
1 cup packed brown sugar
1 cup chopped pecans

Beat the butter, 1/2 cup brown sugar and the granulated sugar in a large bowl until light and fluffy. Add the egg yolks and beat to mix well. Sift the flour, salt and baking soda together. Mix the milk and vanilla in a small bowl. Beat into the sugar mixture alternately with the dry ingredients. Spread the batter in a well-greased 11×16-inch baking pan. Sprinkle with the chocolate chips. Beat the egg whites in a bowl until stiff peaks form. Beat in 1 cup brown sugar gradually. Fold in the pecans carefully. Spread over the batter in the pan. Bake at 350 degrees for 25 minutes or until a wooden pick inserted in the center comes out clean. Remove to a wire rack and let cool before cutting. **Makes 4 to 4 1/2 dozen (1-inch) bars.**

Kahlúa Fudge Bars

$1^{1}/_{2}$ cups sifted all-purpose flour

$^{1}/_{2}$ teaspoon baking powder

$^{1}/_{2}$ teaspoon salt

$10^{2}/_{3}$ tablespoons butter

3 ounces unsweetened chocolate

3 eggs

2 cups sugar

$^{1}/_{4}$ cup Kahlúa

$^{3}/_{4}$ cup chopped pecans

2 tablespoons Kahlúa

Sift the flour, baking powder and salt together. Melt the butter and chocolate in a small saucepan over low heat. Beat the eggs and sugar in a bowl until thick and pale yellow. Beat in the dry ingredients, melted chocolate mixture and $^{1}/_{4}$ cup Kahlúa. Stir in the pecans. Pour into a greased 9×9-inch baking pan lined with foil. Bake at 350 degrees for 35 to 40 minutes or until the top springs back when touched lightly in the center and the edges of the brownie pull away from the pan. Remove to a wire rack and let cool thoroughly. Brush the top with 2 tablespoons Kahlúa. Cut into 1×2-inch bars. **Makes 2 dozen bars.**

Chocolate Peanut Butter Bars

1 cup (2 sticks) butter, softened

1 cup chunky peanut butter

1 (16-ounce) package confectioners' sugar

$1^{1}/_{2}$ cups crushed vanilla wafers

2 cups semisweet chocolate chips

$^{1}/_{2}$ cup heavy cream

Combine the butter and peanut butter in a large bowl. Beat with an electric mixer at medium speed to mix well. Beat in the confectioners' sugar and crushed vanilla wafers. Press into a lightly greased 9×13-inch baking pan lined with waxed paper. Combine the chocolate chips and cream in a saucepan. Cook over low heat until the chocolate melts, stirring constantly. Pour evenly over the peanut butter mixture. Chill for 1 hour. Cut into bars. **Makes 2 dozen bars.**

Vienna Chocolate Bars

1 cup (2 sticks) butter, softened

2 egg yolks

$^1/_2$ cup sugar

$2^1/_2$ cups all-purpose flour

1 (10-ounce) jar raspberry jelly or apricot preserves

1 cup chocolate chips

4 egg whites

$^1/_4$ teaspoon salt

2 cups finely chopped pecans

1 cup sugar

Beat the butter, egg yolks and $^1/_2$ cup sugar in a bowl until light and fluffy. Add the flour and mix with hands to form a dough. Pat onto a greased cookie sheet to $^3/_8$-inch thickness. Bake at 350 degrees for 15 to 20 minutes or until light brown. Spread with the jelly and sprinkle with the chocolate chips. Beat the egg whites and salt in a bowl until stiff peaks form. Fold in the pecans and 1 cup sugar. Spread over the chocolate chips. Bake at 350 degrees for 25 minutes. Remove to a wire rack to cool. Cut into bars or squares. **Makes 30 bars.**

Chocolate Mint Squares

1 cup all-purpose flour

1 cup sugar

1/2 cup (1 stick) butter, softened

4 eggs

1 (16-ounce) can chocolate syrup

2 cups confectioners' sugar

1/2 cup (1 stick) butter, softened

1 tablespoon water

3/4 teaspoon mint extract

Few drops of green food color

1 cup semisweet chocolate chips

6 tablespoons butter

Beat the flour, sugar, 1/2 cup butter, the eggs and chocolate syrup in a large bowl until smooth. Pour into a greased 9×13-inch baking pan. Bake at 350 degrees for 25 to 30 minutes or until a wooden pick inserted in the center comes out clean. Remove to a wire rack to cool completely. Beat the confectioners' sugar, 1/2 cup butter, the water, mint extract and food color in a bowl until smooth. Spread over the cooled baked layer. Combine the chocolate chips and 6 tablespoons butter in a saucepan. Cook until the butter melts and the mixture is smooth, stirring constantly. Remove from the heat and let cool slightly. Spread over the mint layer. Cover and chill. Cut into squares.

Makes 2 dozen squares.

Pecan Squares

2 cups all-purpose flour
$^2/_3$ cup confectioners' sugar
$^3/_4$ cup ($1^1/_2$ sticks) butter, softened
$^1/_2$ cup packed brown sugar
$^1/_2$ cup honey
$^2/_3$ cup butter
3 tablespoons heavy cream
$3^1/_2$ cups coarsely chopped pecans

Sift the flour and confectioners' sugar into a bowl. Cut in $^3/_4$ cup butter with a pastry blender or fork until the mixture resembles coarse meal. Pat onto the bottom and $1^1/_2$ inches up the sides of a lightly greased 9×13-inch baking dish. Bake at 350 degrees for 20 minutes or until the edges are light brown. Remove to a wire rack and let cool. Combine the brown sugar, honey, $^2/_3$ cup butter and the cream in a saucepan. Bring to a boil over medium-high heat. Stir in the pecans. Pour over the prepared crust. Bake at 350 degrees for 25 to 30 minutes or until golden brown and bubbly. Remove to a wire rack to cool completely. Cut into 2-inch squares. **Makes 2 dozen.**

Dipped Shortbread

2 cups all-purpose flour
1 cup (2 sticks) butter, softened
$1/2$ cup confectioners' sugar
1 teaspoon vanilla extract
1 cup semisweet chocolate chips
1 tablespoon shortening
$1/2$ cup finely chopped nuts

Combine the flour, butter, confectioners' sugar and vanilla in a large bowl. Stir to mix well. Shape heaping teaspoonfuls of dough into 2-inch logs and place on an ungreased cookie sheet. Bake at 350 degrees for 10 to 12 minutes. Remove the cookies to a wire rack to cool completely. Melt the chocolate chips and shortening in the top of a double boiler over hot water. Remove from the heat. Dip 1 end of each cookie into the melted chocolate and coat in the nuts. Place on a plate lined with waxed paper. Chill until the chocolate is firm. **Makes 5 dozen cookies.**

Apple Pie in a Paper Bag

2 1/2 pounds Golden Delicious or other baking apples, peeled, cored and cubed

3/4 cup sugar

2 tablespoons all-purpose flour

1 teaspoon cinnamon

1 unbaked (9-inch) deep-dish pie shell

2 tablespoons lemon juice

1/2 cup sugar

1/2 cup all-purpose flour

1/2 cup (1 stick) butter, softened

Combine the apples, 3/4 cup sugar, 2 tablespoons flour and the cinnamon in a large bowl. Toss to mix. Spoon into the pie shell. Sprinkle with the lemon juice. Mix 1/2 cup sugar and 1/2 cup flour in a bowl. Cut in the butter with a pastry blender or fork until crumbly. Sprinkle over the apples. Place the pie in a large heavy nonrecycled brown paper bag. Fold the end over and secure with paper clips. Place on a baking sheet. Bake at 425 degrees for 1 hour. Remove from the oven and cut open the bag with scissors. Remove the pie to a wire rack and let cool. **Serves 8.**

Coconut Macadamia Nut Pie

1 (1-crust) refrigerator pie pastry

1 cup sugar

1 cup light corn syrup

1 tablespoon butter, melted

3 eggs

$^{1}/_{4}$ cup heavy cream

1 teaspoon vanilla extract

$^{3}/_{4}$ cup coarsely chopped macadamia nuts

1 cup flaked coconut

Fit the pastry into a 9-inch pie plate. Freeze for 15 minutes. Bake at 425 degrees for 6 to 8 minutes or until golden brown. Remove to a wire rack and let cool. Whisk the sugar, corn syrup, melted butter, eggs, cream and vanilla in a bowl. Stir in the macadamia nuts and coconut. Pour into the baked crust. Bake at 350 degrees for 55 to 60 minutes. Remove to a wire rack to cool. Garnish with whipped cream, chopped macadamia nuts and toasted flaked coconut, if desired. **Serves 8.**

Coconut Cream Pie

$3/4$ cup sugar

$1/4$ cup cornstarch

$1/8$ teaspoon salt

3 cups milk

3 egg yolks, beaten

$1/2$ cup flaked coconut

$1^1/2$ tablespoons butter or margarine

1 teaspoon vanilla extract

1 baked (9-inch) pie shell

3 egg whites

$1/4$ teaspoon plus $1/8$ teaspoon cream of tartar

6 tablespoons sugar

$1/4$ cup flaked coconut

Mix $3/4$ cup sugar, the cornstarch and salt in a heavy saucepan. Mix the milk and egg yolks in a bowl. Stir into the sugar mixture gradually. Cook over medium heat until the mixture thickens and boils, stirring constantly. Cook for 1 minute, stirring constantly. Remove from the heat and stir in $1/2$ cup coconut, the butter and vanilla. Pour into the pie shell. Cover the filling with waxed paper. Combine the egg whites and cream of tartar in a bowl. Beat with an electric mixer at high speed for 1 minute. Beat in 6 tablespoons sugar, 1 tablespoon at a time. Beat for 2 to 4 minutes or until stiff peaks form and the sugar dissolves. Remove the waxed paper from the filling. Spread the meringue over the hot filling. Sprinkle with $1/4$ cup coconut. Bake at 350 degrees for 12 to 15 minutes or until golden brown and the egg white is cooked through. Remove to a wire rack to cool. Store in the refrigerator. **Serves 8.**

German Chocolate Pie

4 ounces German's sweet chocolate	2 eggs
1/4 cup (1/2 stick) butter	1 teaspoon vanilla extract
1 1/3 cups evaporated milk	1 unbaked (9- or 10-inch) pie shell
1 1/2 cups sugar	1 1/3 cups flaked coconut
3 tablespoons cornstarch	1/2 cup pecans, chopped
1/8 teaspoon salt	

Melt the chocolate and butter in a saucepan over low heat. Stir in the evaporated milk gradually. Remove from the heat. Mix the sugar, cornstarch and salt in a large bowl. Mix the eggs and vanilla in a bowl. Stir into the sugar mixture. Stir in the chocolate mixture gradually. Pour into the pie shell. Mix the coconut and pecans in a bowl. Sprinkle over the filling. Bake at 375 degrees for 45 to 50 minutes. Do not overbake; the filling should still be soft in the center. Remove to a wire rack to cool. Serve with whipped cream or ice cream. **Serves 8.**

Note: This can be made 1 day ahead. Cover and chill.

Texas Chocolate Pecan Pie

1 cup sugar	2 teaspoons vanilla extract
1 cup light corn syrup	1 cup pecans
3 eggs	1/2 cup chocolate chips
2 tablespoons butter, melted	1 unbaked (9-inch) pie shell

Beat the sugar, corn syrup, eggs, melted butter and vanilla in a large bowl. Stir in the pecans and chocolate chips. Pour into the pie shell. Cover the edges of the crust with foil to prevent excess browning. Bake at 350 degrees for 55 to 60 minutes or until a knife inserted in the center comes out clean. Remove to a wire rack to cool. Serve with ice cream or whipped cream. **Serves 8.**

Chocolate Toffee Pie

1 package graham crackers, crushed

$1/2$ cup (1 stick) margarine, melted

1 cup semisweet chocolate chips

$1/4$ cup ($1/2$ stick) margarine

$1/4$ cup light corn syrup

2 teaspoons water

32 marshmallows

$1/3$ cup milk

4 (1-ounce) chocolate-covered toffee candy bars, broken into pieces

1 cup heavy cream

3 tablespoons chopped toasted almonds

Combine the crushed graham crackers and $1/2$ cup melted margarine in a bowl. Mix with a fork. Press into a 9-inch pie plate and chill. Combine the chocolate chips, $1/4$ cup margarine and the corn syrup in a saucepan. Cook over low heat until the chocolate melts, stirring constantly. Remove from the heat and let cool slightly. Stir in the water, 1 teaspoon at a time. Pour into the crust and chill for 1 hour. Combine the marshmallows and milk in the top of a double boiler. Cook over hot water until the marshmallows melt, stirring occasionally. Remove from the heat and add the candy pieces. Stir until the candy partially melts. Chill until thickened but not set. Beat the cream in a bowl until thickened. Fold gently into the marshmallow mixture. Spoon over the chocolate layer in the pie crust. Chill for 3 hours. Sprinkle with the almonds. **Serves 8.**

Cappuccino Ice Cream Pie

18 chocolate sandwich cookies, crushed
2 tablespoons butter, melted
1 quart coffee ice cream, softened
1 cup heavy cream, whipped
2 tablespoons Kahlúa
Hot Fudge Topping (below)

Mix the crushed cookies and melted butter in a bowl. Press into a springform pan and chill. Mix the ice cream, whipped cream and Kahlúa in a bowl. Pour evenly over the chilled crust. Freeze until firm. Spread warm Hot Fudge Topping over the top and refreeze. Loosen from the side of the pan with a sharp knife and remove the side. Place on a serving plate. Serve with additional whipped cream, if desired. **Serves 8.**

Hot Fudge Topping

2 ounces unsweetened chocolate
1/4 cup (1/2 stick) butter
1/4 cup baking cocoa
3/4 cup sugar
3/4 cup evaporated milk
1 teaspoon vanilla extract

Melt the chocolate and butter in a saucepan over low heat. Remove from the heat and whisk in the baking cocoa until smooth. Stir in the sugar and evaporated milk. Bring to a boil slowly, stirring constantly. Remove from the heat and stir in the vanilla. Beat for 2 minutes. Let stand until warm.

Simply Delicious Ice Cream Pie

1 (24-ounce) package ice cream sandwiches
10 miniature chocolate-covered toffee candy bars, chopped,
    or 1 (8-ounce) package chocolate-covered toffee bits
1 (16-ounce) container frozen whipped topping, thawed
Chocolate syrup

Fit the ice cream sandwiches into a 9×13-inch baking dish. Sprinkle with $1/2$ of the chopped candy. Spread the whipped topping over the candy. Drizzle chocolate syrup over the whipped topping and sprinkle with the remaining candy. Freeze until firm. Let stand at room temperature for 20 minutes before serving. **Serves 8 to12.**

Irish Cream Pies

    5 eggs
    1$^{1}/_{4}$ cups sugar
    $^{1}/_{2}$ teaspoon salt
    $^{3}/_{4}$ cup (1$^{1}/_{2}$ sticks) butter, melted
    1 cup corn syrup
    $^{3}/_{4}$ cup Irish cream liqueur
    1$^{1}/_{3}$ cups chocolate chips
    6 ounces macadamia nuts, chopped
    2 (9-inch) vanilla wafer pie shells

Beat the eggs, sugar, salt and melted butter in a bowl. Stir in the corn syrup and liqueur. Stir in the chocolate chips and macadamia nuts. Pour into the pie shells. Bake at 300 degrees for 1$^{1}/_{2}$ to 2 hours. Remove to a wire rack to cool. **Serves 16.**

Apple Sin (Eve's Delight)

1 (2-layer) package butter-recipe cake mix
1/2 cup flaked coconut
1/2 cup (1 stick) butter, melted
1 (21-ounce) can apple pie filling
1 egg
1 cup sour cream
1/2 cup sugar
1 teaspoon cinnamon

Combine the cake mix, coconut and melted butter in a bowl. Stir to mix well. Press into a greased 9×13-inch baking pan. Bake at 350 degrees for 10 minutes. Spread the pie filling over the baked crust. Mix the egg and sour cream in a small bowl. Drizzle over the pie filling. Mix the sugar and cinnamon in a small bowl and sprinkle over the top. Bake at 350 degrees for 25 minutes. Remove to a wire rack. Serve warm with vanilla ice cream. **Serves 12 to 16.**

Nutty Caramel Wedges

1 (1-crust) refrigerator pie pastry

$^3/_4$ cup regular or fat-free caramel ice cream topping

2 eggs

2 tablespoons butter, melted

1 teaspoon vanilla extract

1 (10-ounce) can salted mixed nuts

Line a 9-inch round cake pan with foil, leaving 2 inches to extend above the rim. Fit the pastry into the pan, folding down the top edge to extend 1 inch above the rim. Press the edge gently with a fork. Prick the pastry with a fork. Press a sheet of foil firmly into the pastry. Bake at 450 degrees for 12 minutes. Remove the sheet of foil and bake for 6 minutes longer or until light brown. Remove to a wire rack. Whisk the caramel topping, eggs, melted butter and vanilla in a bowl. Pour into the baked crust. Sprinkle with the nuts. Bake at 350 degrees for 25 to 30 minutes or until puffed and a knife inserted in the center comes out clean. Remove to a wire rack and let cool. Chill for at least 4 hours. Lift by the edge of the foil to remove from the pan to a cutting board. Cut into 24 wedges. **Serves 24.**

Holiday Cheesecake

1 cup finely ground cashews

1 sleeve (18 squares) graham crackers, finely crushed

$1/2$ cup sugar

$1/2$ cup (1 stick) butter, melted

32 ounces cream cheese, softened

1 cup sugar

1 tablespoon rum, or 1 teaspoon rum flavoring

1 teaspoon vanilla extract

$1/2$ teaspoon nutmeg

3 eggs

$1^1/2$ cups eggnog

Mix the cashews, crushed graham crackers and $1/2$ cup sugar in a bowl. Add the melted butter and stir to mix well. Press onto the bottom and $1^1/2$ inches up the side of a 10-inch springform pan. Wrap the outside of the pan tightly with heavy-duty foil. Beat the cream cheese in a large bowl with an electric mixer at medium-high speed for 3 to 4 minutes. Beat in 1 cup sugar gradually. Beat for 2 to 3 minutes or until very smooth, scraping down the side as needed. Reduce the speed to medium and beat in the rum, vanilla and nutmeg. Add the eggs and beat at low speed just until combined. Stir in the eggnog. Pour into the prepared crust. Place the springform pan in a large roasting pan. Add enough very hot water to the larger pan to come halfway up the side of the springform pan. Bake at 350 degrees for 60 to 70 minutes or until the center is almost set. Remove the springform pan to a wire rack and let cool for 15 minutes. Remove the foil outer covering. Loosen from the side of the pan with a sharp knife. Let cool for 30 minutes. Remove the side of the pan and let cool for 1 hour. Cover and chill for at least 8 hours. **Serves 16.**

Pumpkin Cheesecake

$^1/_2$ cup graham cracker crumbs

$^1/_4$ cup finely crushed gingersnaps

2 tablespoons finely chopped pecans

1 tablespoon all-purpose flour

1 tablespoon confectioners' sugar

2 tablespoons butter, melted

16 ounces cream cheese, softened

1 cup granulated sugar

3 eggs

1 (15-ounce) can pumpkin

1 egg

$^1/_4$ cup milk

$^1/_2$ teaspoon cinnamon

$^1/_4$ teaspoon ginger

$^1/_4$ teaspoon nutmeg

Whipped cream

Toasted chopped pecans

Combine the graham cracker crumbs, crushed gingersnaps, pecans, flour, confectioners' sugar and butter in a bowl. Stir to mix well. Press onto the bottom of a 9-inch springform pan. Combine the cream cheese and granulated sugar in a large bowl. Beat with an electric mixer at medium speed until light and fluffy. Add 3 eggs and beat at low speed just until combined. Remove 1 cup of the cream cheese mixture to a bowl. Add the pumpkin, 1 egg, the milk, cinnamon, ginger and nutmeg. Beat with an electric mixer at low speed just until combined. Pour the pumpkin mixture into the prepared crust. Top with the cream cheese mixture. Swirl gently through the layers with a knife. Place the springform pan in a shallow baking pan. Bake at 350 degrees for 40 to 45 minutes or until the center appears set when gently shaken. Remove the springform pan to a wire rack and let cool for 15 minutes. Loosen from the side of the pan with a sharp knife. Let cool for 30 minutes. Remove the side of the pan and let cool completely. Cover and chill for at least 4 hours. Serve topped with whipped cream and chopped pecans. **Serves 12 to 16.**

Death-by-Chocolate Trifle

1 (2-layer) package chocolate cake mix,
   batter prepared according to the package directions
1 cup Kahlúa
4 (3-ounce) packages chocolate instant pudding mix,
   prepared according to the package directions
1 (16-ounce) container frozen whipped topping, thawed
6 chocolate-covered toffee candy bars, chopped

Pour the cake batter into a greased 9×13-inch cake pan. Bake according to the package directions. Remove to a wire rack. Poke holes in the top of the cake with a fork. Pour the Kahlúa evenly over the hot cake. Let cool completely. Crumble or cut the cake into small pieces. Place 1/2 of the cake in a trifle bowl or glass serving bowl. Top with 1/2 of the prepared pudding and spread 1/2 of the whipped topping over the pudding. Sprinkle with 1/2 of the candy. Repeat the layers. Cover and chill until cold. **Serves 12.**

Frozen Raspberry Chocolate Dessert

$1^1/2$ packages chocolate graham crackers, crushed

$^1/4$ cup confectioners' sugar

$^1/4$ cup ($^1/2$ stick) butter or margarine, melted

2 pints raspberry sherbet or sorbet, slightly softened

1 (8-ounce) jar hot fudge sauce

1 (16-ounce) container frozen whipped topping, thawed

$^1/2$ cup chocolate sauce

Combine the crushed graham crackers, confectioners' sugar and butter in a bowl. Stir to mix well. Press into a buttered springform pan. Bake at 350 degrees for 10 minutes. Remove to a wire rack to cool completely. Spoon the sherbet evenly into the cooled crust and top with the hot fudge sauce. Mix $^1/2$ of the whipped topping and the chocolate sauce in a bowl. Spread over the hot fudge sauce. Top with the remaining whipped topping. Freeze until firm. **Serves 8.**

Note: Strained, puréed frozen raspberries make a nice sauce to serve with this dessert.

Big Red Ice Cream

3 bananas, mashed
1 (8-ounce) can crushed pineapple
2 (14-ounce) cans sweetened
   condensed milk

1 (15-ounce) package frozen
   strawberries, thawed
28 ounces Big Red soda

Mix the bananas, pineapple, sweetened condensed milk and strawberries in a bowl.
Pour into an ice cream freezer container. Add the soda. Freeze using the manufacturer's
directions. **Serves 15.**

Simply the Best Banana Pudding

1 cup sugar
$1/3$ cup sifted all-purpose flour
$1/2$ teaspoon salt
3 egg yolks
2 cups milk
$1/2$ cup evaporated milk
1 tablespoon butter

1 teaspoon vanilla extract
3 egg whites
6 tablespoons sugar
1 cup heavy whipping cream, whipped
Dash of vanilla extract
Vanilla wafers
4 bananas, sliced

Mix 1 cup sugar, the flour and salt in a saucepan. Stir in the egg yolks, milk, evaporated
milk, butter and 1 teaspoon vanilla. Bring to a boil and cook until thick, stirring often.
Remove from the heat and cool completely. Beat the egg whites and 6 tablespoons
sugar in a bowl until stiff peaks form. Fold in the whipped cream and a dash of vanilla.
Arrange a layer of vanilla wafers in a serving bowl. Top with $1/2$ of the pudding. Arrange
$1/2$ of the banana slices on the pudding. Cover with $1/2$ of the whipped cream mixture.
Repeat the layers. Cover and chill until cold. **Serves 6 to 8.**

Note: If you are concerned about using raw eggs, use eggs pasteurized in their shells,
which are sold at some specialty food stores, or use equivalent amounts of pasteurized
egg substitute and meringue powder.

Layered Almond Cream Cheese Bread Pudding

1 (16-ounce) loaf sliced honey white bread	2 teaspoons vanilla extract
8 ounces cream cheese, softened	$2^1/2$ cups half-and-half
1 egg	Dash of salt
$1/4$ cup sugar	1 egg yolk
1 teaspoon vanilla extract	$1/2$ cup (1 stick) butter, melted
$1^1/4$ cups canned almond filling	2 tablespoons canned almond filling
$1/2$ cup (1 stick) butter, melted	2 tablespoons sugar
8 eggs	$1/4$ cup slivered almonds
	Amaretto Cream Sauce (below)

Fit $4^1/2$ bread slices into a 9×13-inch baking pan coated with nonstick cooking spray, cutting the bread if necessary to fit. Beat the cream cheese, 1 egg, $1/4$ cup sugar and 1 teaspoon vanilla in a bowl until smooth. Spread half the cream cheese mixture over the bread slices in the baking pan. Whisk $1^1/4$ cups almond filling and $1/2$ cup butter in a bowl. Spread half over the cream cheese mixture in the baking pan. Repeat the layers, using $4^1/2$ bread slices and the remaining cream cheese and almond mixtures. Cut the remaining bread into 1-inch cubes and sprinkle over the top. Whisk 8 eggs, 2 teaspoons vanilla, the half-and-half and salt in a bowl. Pour over the bread cubes. Cover and chill until most of the liquid is absorbed. Whisk the egg yolk, $1/2$ cup butter, 2 tablespoons almond filling and 2 tablespoons sugar in a bowl. Drizzle over the bread pudding. Sprinkle with the almonds. Bake at 325 degrees for 1 hour or until set. Remove to a wire rack. Serve warm or chilled with the Amaretto Cream Sauce. **Serves 12.**

Amaretto Cream Sauce

$1/2$ cup amaretto	$1^1/2$ cups heavy cream
2 tablespoons cornstarch	$1/2$ cup sugar

Mix the liqueur and cornstarch in a small bowl. Heat the cream in a heavy saucepan over medium heat until bubbles appear, stirring frequently. Stir in the liqueur mixture gradually. Bring to a boil over medium heat. Boil for 30 seconds, stirring constantly. Remove from the heat and add the sugar. Stir until the sugar dissolves. Let cool.

Pumpkin Pie Crunch Dessert

1 (16-ounce) can pumpkin

1 (12-ounce) can evaporated milk

3 eggs

1 1/2 cups sugar

2 1/2 teaspoons cinnamon

1 teaspoon ginger

1/2 teaspoon cloves

1/2 teaspoon salt

1 (2-layer) package butter-recipe cake mix

1 cup chopped pecans

1 cup (2 sticks) butter, melted

Whipped Topping (below)

Combine the pumpkin, evaporated milk, eggs, sugar, cinnamon, ginger, cloves and salt in a large bowl. Stir to mix well. Pour into a nonstick 9×13-inch baking pan. Sprinkle the dry cake mix evenly over the top. Sprinkle with the pecans and drizzle with the melted butter. Bake at 350 degrees for 50 to 60 minutes or until golden brown. Remove to a wire rack to cool. Serve with the Whipped Topping. **Serves 12.**

Whipped Topping

1 cup heavy whipping cream

1 1/2 teaspoons vanilla extract

2 tablespoons sugar

1 to 2 teaspoons cinnamon

Beat the cream, vanilla, sugar and cinnamon in a bowl until soft peaks form.

Caramel Pecan Topping for Apple Pie

$^1/4$ cup ($^1/2$ stick) butter

$^1/2$ cup packed brown sugar

2 tablespoons heavy cream

$^1/2$ cup chopped pecans

Combine the butter, brown sugar and cream in a heavy saucepan. Bring to a boil slowly, stirring constantly. Remove from the heat and stir in the pecans. Pour over the top of a prepared apple pie. Serve warm with vanilla ice cream. **Makes 1 cup.**

Note: This is also good over brownies.

Broussard Sauce for Strawberries

4 ounces cream cheese, softened

$^1/2$ cup plus 2 tablespoons sugar

$^1/2$ cup half-and-half

1$^1/2$ tablespoons vanilla extract

Beat the cream cheese and sugar in a bowl until light and fluffy. Beat in the half-and-half and vanilla. Chill for at least 30 minutes. Serve over strawberries. **Makes 1$^3/4$ cups.**

Mocha Chocolate Sauce

$1/2$ cup heavy cream

2 cups chocolate chips

2 tablespoons honey

2 tablespoons brewed coffee

Combine the cream and chocolate chips in the top of a double boiler. Cook over simmering water until the chocolate melts, stirring often. Add the honey and coffee and stir to mix. Serve over ice cream or cake with fruit. **Makes 1$1/4$ cups.**

Praline Ice Cream Sauce

1 cup packed dark brown sugar

$1/4$ cup light corn syrup

$1/2$ cup evaporated milk

2 tablespoons butter

1 teaspoon vanilla extract

$1/8$ teaspoon salt

1 cup coarsely chopped pecans

Combine the brown sugar, corn syrup, evaporated milk, butter, vanilla, salt and pecans in a saucepan. Cook over medium heat for 10 minutes or until thick, stirring constantly. Remove from the heat and let cool slightly. Serve over vanilla ice cream. **Makes 2 cups.**

Raspberry-Mandarin Sundae Sauce

1 (15¹/4-ounce) jar seedless fruit-only raspberry jam

3 tablespoons orange liqueur or orange juice

1 (11-ounce) can mandarin oranges packed
    in light syrup, drained

Whisk the jam in a bowl until smooth. Stir in the liqueur. Stir in the oranges gently. Serve immediately over ice cream or store in an airtight container in the refrigerator for up to 1 week. **Makes 2¹/2 cups.**

Acknowledgments

The cookbook committee wishes to thank the members of the Rockwall Women's League who submitted, reviewed, tested, and proofread recipes. We also gratefully recognize the creativity, talent, and dedication of all who supported this cookbook project.

Dottie Abernathy
Lee Albright
Vicki Alexander
Barbara Allan
Monika Amick
Sherry Anderson
Teresa Andrews
Nancy Archibald
Laurie Arterburn
Beth Bailey
Kathie Bailey
Debbie Ballard
Barbara Baumann
Shawn Baxter
Jennifer Bayoud
Lucille Bell
Cindy Bledsoe
Kathy Bookhout
Andrea Burke
Linda Burns
Tina Caldwell
Gail Caruth
Jean Chaplin

Susan Clevenger
Terri Coleman
Barbara Coleson
Natalie Colon
Debbie Cullins
Debbie Daniels
Jennifer Davenport
Patty Davis
Sue Davis
Gay Diamond
Sherry Dickerson
Kim Dobbs
Donna Duhon
Julie Edwards
Joanne Efeney
Helen Elkins
Dee Evans
Kathleen Evans
Kim Fisher
Alison Fox
Sheri Franza
Judy Freese
Carolyn Gehring

Marcia Gilbert
Rosemary Goodman
Joey Grand-Lienard
Shelle Graves
Mary Kay Griffin
Karen Hall
Randa Hance
Claudette Hatfield
Maggie Hatfield
Corleen Helwig
Patsy Hendrickson
Stephanie Holden
Melissa Holland
Melissa Holliman
Lynn Houston
Alma Williams Howard
Cristi Hudecek
Sheri Hughes
Susie Hughes
Toni Humes
Bobbie Johnson
Carlil Johnson
Lisa Johnson

Tish Johnson
Tonya Jost
Glenda Kelldorf
Ann Kenney
Paula Kerr
Jeannette Keton
Marilyn King
Jennifer Lamberth
Jean Lewis
Stacy Loeffler
Chrissie Loftis
Lisa Long
Lynn Lowry
Tome Martin
Margaret Mayo
Brenda Meyers
Allyson Minth
Judy Minth
Kristen Minth
Betty Moon
Sharon Moon
Marla Moser
Joyce Musser

Catherine Night
Charlene Norris
Muriel Osborne
Jinksie Patton
Deloris Petty
Keli Phillips
Phyllis Pierce
Sue Pirtle
Patti Poole
Julie Fuller Pratt
Patsy Pratt
Palmer Ragsdale
Robin Railsback
Cathy Raney
Susan Robinson
Judy Rogers
Ruth Ruhl
Susan Satterwhite
Judy Schneider
Cynthia Seay
Freda Sexton
Janet Smith
Kay Loy Smith

Peg Pannell Smith
Michelle Sorrells
Mary South
Connie Stewart
Kim Story
Karen Sturgeon
Elaine Sullivan
Paula Talley
Suzanne Talley
Christine Tarski
M. Joan Terry
Linda Thompson
Wendy Thompson
Kim Turner
Nancy Underwood
Kim Wallen
Lisa Ward
Frankie White
Leigh Wilcoxson
Lisa Willis
Phuong Willis
Alisa Wimpee
Peggy Wyatt

Sponsors

The Rockwall Women's League appreciates these loyal sponsors for their generous financial support of *A League of Our Own* before it was ever published.

In honor of Greg Alexander, my favorite chef
– Vicki Alexander

In memory of Beatrice and Inga
– Patsy and Don Hendrickson

Kim and Calvin Wallen III

In honor of Mary Kay Griffin
– Elaine Sullivan

In honor of my mother, Marilyn Steen
– Stephanie Holden

In honor of my mom, Marilyn, and Uncle Bob
– Monika Amick

Glenn and Blair Baldwin

We love you, Mary Kay. (P.S. What's for dinner?)
– Dave, Erin, and D.J. Griffin

In honor of my parent's 50th Wedding Anniversary 5-12-05
– Peg Pannell Smith

Mark and Leigh Wilcoxson

In honor of my students
– *Gail Caruth*

Kim and Preston Dobbs

In honor of my clients
– *Dee Evans*

In honor of my lifelong
friends in RWL
– *Kathleen Evans*

In honor of my 2004-05
Executive Board
– *Alison Fox*

In honor of all RWL Presidents
(especially the first) and
Ball Chairs
– *Mary Kay Griffin*

Claudette and Honey,
we love you with all our hearts
– *Maggie Hatfield and
Susan Wheelis*

In honor of my first influence as
a cook, my great-grandmother,
Ollie Edgington
– *Melissa Holliman*

In memory of Ella Troster
– *Lynn Houston*

In honor of Cora Reynolds
– *Brent, Cristi, Mike, Caitlin,
and Joshua Hudecek*

In loving memory of my
Daddy and my Father-in-Law
– *Carlil Johnson*

With love to our grandchildren,
John and Gracie
– *John and Marilyn King*

In honor of my friend,
Sheri Hughes
– *Allyson Minth*

For my friend and mother,
Judy Minth
– *Kristen Minth*

In honor of great cooks,
Lydia, Doris, Kitty, and Sarah
– *Scott and Cathy Night*

In honor of our mothers,
Carolyn and Nanette
– *Scott and Cathy Night*

Patti and Ben Poole

In honor of
Patsy Hendrickson and
Alma Howard
– *Love, Susan Robinson*

Rockwall MusicFest

In honor of our favorite
Associate, Paula Talley
– *Doug and Suzanne Talley*

In honor of my friends,
the precious gems of RWL
– *Phuong Willis*

Index

A League of Our Own

Rockwall Women's League
Attention: Cookbook Chairman
P.O. Box 383
Rockwall, Texas 75087

Name _____

Street Address _____

City   State   Zip Code _____

Your Order	Qty	Total
A League of Our Own at $19.95 per book		$
Texas residents please add 8.25% sales tax at $1.65 per book		$
Shipping and handling at $3.00 per book		$
Total		$

Method of Payment: [   ] VISA   [   ] MasterCard
[   ] Check made payable to Rockwall Women's League

Account Number _____   Expiration Date _____

Cardholder Name _____

Signature _____

Order online at: www.rockwallwomensleague.org

Proceeds from the sale of this cookbook will be returned to the community through projects and organizations supported by the Rockwall Women's League.

Photocopies accepted

Thank you for your order!